HOW TO MANAGE YOUR MONEY LIKE A MILLIONAIRE

JOY DANIELS

Copyright © 2024 by Joy Daniels

All rights reserved. No part of this book may be reproduced, stored in a retrieval system, or transmitted, in any form or by any means, electronic, mechanical, photocopying, recording, or otherwise, without the prior written permission of the author, except in the case of brief quotations embodied in critical reviews and certain other noncommercial uses permitted by copyright law.

TABLE OF CONTENT

INTRODUCTION

Are you tired of living paycheck to paycheck, constantly stressed about your finances? Do you dream of a life where money is no longer a source of worry but a tool to fulfil your wildest aspirations? Look no further! In "How to Manage Your Money Like a Millionaire," we unveil the secrets that millionaires use to not only amass great wealth but also sustain and grow it over time.

Unlock the Millionaire Mindset

Ever wondered what sets millionaires apart from the rest of us? It's not just luck or inheritance; it's a mindset—a way of thinking about and managing money that propels them toward success. In this book, we delve deep into the millionaire mindset, teaching you how to cultivate it for yourself. Learn how to visualize your financial goals, overcome limiting beliefs, and develop the confidence to make decisions that will transform your financial future.

Create Your Financial Blueprint

No journey is successful without a map, and your financial journey is no exception. "How to Manage Your Money Like a Millionaire" provides you with a step-by-step guide to creating your personalized financial blueprint. From setting achievable short-term goals to crafting a long-term strategy for financial independence, this book empowers you to take control of your financial destiny.

Master the Art of Budgeting and Saving

Budgeting doesn't mean sacrificing your lifestyle; it means allocating your resources wisely. Discover the art of creating a realistic budget that allows you to enjoy life while still building wealth. Learn how to save strategically, invest wisely, and make your money work for you. With practical tips and real-life examples, you'll be on your way to financial freedom sooner than you think.

Navigate the World of Investments

Millionaires understand the power of investments, and so should you. Whether you're a seasoned investor or just starting, this book provides insights into the various investment options available and helps you determine which ones align with your financial goals. From stocks and bonds to real estate and entrepreneurship, uncover the secrets of building a diversified and lucrative investment portfolio.

Crush Debt and Supercharge Your Wealth

Debt can be a roadblock to financial success, but it doesn't have to be a permanent fixture in your life. "How to Manage Your Money Like a Millionaire" equips you with proven strategies to eliminate debt efficiently and pave the way for building substantial wealth. Say goodbye to financial stress and hello to a life of abundance.

Cultivate a Legacy of Prosperity

True financial success isn't just about accumulating wealth for yourself; it's about creating a lasting legacy for future generations. Learn how millionaires approach estate planning, philanthropy, and generational wealth transfer. Discover the joy of making a positive impact on the world while securing a prosperous future for your loved ones.

If you're ready to transform your relationship with money and live a life of abundance, "How to Manage Your Money like a Millionaire" is your roadmap to financial success. Start your journey today and unlock the doors to a future where financial freedom is not just a dream but a reality waiting to be embraced.

CHAPTER 1: UNVEILING THE MILLIONAIRE MINDSET

Welcome to the gateway of financial transformation. In this chapter, we embark on a journey to unravel the enigma that separates the financially successful from the rest—the elusive but tangible concept known as the "Millionaire Mindset." Beyond the bank accounts and investment portfolios lies a mindset, a set of principles and beliefs that propels individuals toward not just monetary success, but enduring wealth.

Have you ever wondered why some people seem to effortlessly attract prosperity while others grapple with financial stress? It's not about luck or coincidence; it's about mindset—the way we think about money, success, and our potential. In the pages that follow, we will dissect the elements of the Millionaire Mindset, unveiling the secrets that have empowered individuals to transcend financial limitations and achieve extraordinary success.

Our exploration begins with understanding the psychology of wealth. We will delve into the power of positive thinking, the art of overcoming limiting beliefs, and the transformative force of visualizing financial success. Through real-life examples and actionable insights, you will gain the tools needed to reshape your mindset and pave the way for a future where financial abundance is not just a distant dream but an achievable reality.

But the Millionaire Mindset is more than just positive thinking; it's about cultivating financial confidence. In the face of challenges, setbacks, and risks, millionaires possess a unique resilience and a can-do attitude that propels them forward. We will explore how you can develop this confidence within yourself, enabling you to navigate the financial landscape with assurance and poise.

As we progress, envision your potential. Picture a life where financial worries dissipate, where goals become milestones, and where success is not just a destination but a continuous journey. The Millionaire Mindset is not an exclusive club—it's a mindset waiting to be embraced by those who dare to dream big and work towards their aspirations.

So, let the journey begin. Unveil the Millionaire Mindset within you and discover the keys to unlocking the door to financial success. As we navigate the landscape of mindset, belief, and confidence, remember that the power to shape your financial destiny lies not in external circumstances but in the very core of your being. Are you ready to unleash the wealth within? The adventure starts now.

- The Psychology of Wealth

In the intricate tapestry of financial success, the thread of psychology weaves a pattern that distinguishes the affluent from the financially constrained. Understanding the psychology of wealth is the foundational step towards embracing the Millionaire Mindset—a mindset that transcends material possessions and delves into the core principles that guide financial triumph.

The Power of Positive Thinking

At the heart of the Millionaire Mindset is an unwavering belief in the power of positive thinking. It's more than a cliché; it's a proven force that shapes the trajectory of financial success. This section explores how cultivating optimism and fostering a positive outlook can influence financial decisions, attract opportunities, and set the stage for prosperity.

- Optimism as a Catalyst: Examining how maintaining a positive perspective can fuel resilience in the face of challenges, turning obstacles into stepping stones towards financial success.

- The Law of Attraction: Delving into the concept that like attracts like, exploring how positive thoughts can manifest positive outcomes in one's financial journey.

Overcoming Limiting Beliefs

We all carry beliefs about money—some empowering, others limiting. This section shines a spotlight on identifying and dismantling limiting beliefs that hinder financial growth. Readers will discover strategies to reframe their mindset, break free from self-imposed limitations, and adopt a mindset aligned with abundance.

- **Identifying Limiting Beliefs:** Uncovering common beliefs that hinder financial progress and recognizing their impact on decision-making.

- **Reforming Belief Systems:** Providing practical techniques to rewire thought patterns and replace limiting beliefs with empowering ones.

Visualizing Financial Success

The mind is a powerful tool, and in this section, we explore the transformative practice of visualizing financial success. From creating vivid mental images of prosperity to mapping out future achievements, readers will learn how visualization acts as a catalyst for turning dreams into tangible financial goals.

- **The Art of Visualization:** Exploring techniques to vividly imagine and emotionally connect with future financial successes.

- Creating a Vision Board: Implementing a tangible tool for visualizing goals and reinforcing the commitment to financial aspirations.

As we traverse the psychology of wealth, the aim is not only to uncover the secrets of the Millionaire Mindset but to equip readers with actionable insights that can be applied immediately. By the end of this section, readers will be armed with the knowledge to reshape their thoughts, beliefs, and perceptions about wealth—a powerful foundation for the transformative journey that lies ahead. The Millionaire Mindset begins with the power of the mind, and the psychology of wealth is the key to unlocking its full potential.

- The Power of Positive Thinking

In the grand tapestry of financial success, the brushstroke that colors the canvas is the relentless optimism encapsulated in the power of positive thinking. This section explores the profound impact that maintaining a positive mindset can have on one's financial journey, unravelling the secrets of the Millionaire Mindset that turn challenges into triumphs.

Optimism as a Catalyst

Unleashing Resilience in the Face of Challenges:

The journey toward financial success is inevitably dotted with challenges, setbacks, and unforeseen obstacles. Here, we delve into how adopting a positive outlook acts as a powerful catalyst for resilience. Instead of viewing challenges as insurmountable roadblocks, positive thinking transforms them into opportunities for growth and innovation.

Attracting Financial Opportunities:

The law of attraction posits that positive thoughts attract positive outcomes. We explore how cultivating optimism can create a magnetic field of opportunities, drawing favorable circumstances into one's financial orbit. From career advancements to investment prospects, the mindset of positivity becomes a beacon guiding individuals toward financial success.

The Law of Attraction

Manifesting Wealth Through Positive Thoughts:

The Law of Attraction operates on the principle that thoughts become reality. In this segment, we delve into how consciously directing thoughts toward financial abundance can manifest tangible wealth. By understanding the interplay between thoughts and outcomes, readers will learn to align their mindset with the financial success they aspire to achieve.

Shaping Financial Behavior:

Positive thinking is not merely wishful dreaming; it influences actions and decisions. We explore how a positive mindset shapes financial behavior, fostering discipline, and motivating constructive financial habits. By cultivating an optimistic approach, individuals are better equipped to make informed choices that contribute to long-term financial well-being.

In essence, the power of positive thinking transcends mere optimism—it becomes a force that propels individuals forward in their financial journey. This section is not a call for blind positivity but a strategic approach to viewing challenges as opportunities and consciously directing thoughts toward prosperity. As readers internalize the principles of positive thinking, they lay the foundation for a mindset that not only withstands the storms of financial life but also steers the ship toward the shores of enduring success. The Millionaire Mindset, rooted in optimism, becomes a guiding light, illuminating the path to financial prosperity.

- Overcoming Limiting Beliefs

In the labyrinth of the mind, beliefs are the architects of reality. This section is a compass for navigating the terrain of limiting beliefs, uncovering the barriers that hinder financial growth, and providing a roadmap for readers to overcome these mental constraints on their journey to embracing the Millionaire Mindset.

Identifying Limiting Beliefs

Recognizing the Chains:

Limiting beliefs often lurks in the shadows, shaping our perceptions and influencing decisions without our conscious awareness. In this phase, we embark on a self-discovery journey, unravelling the deep-seated beliefs that act as invisible chains restraining financial potential. Through reflective exercises and insightful prompts, readers learn to identify these beliefs and acknowledge their impact.

Common Financial Limitations:

Exploring the prevalent limiting beliefs related to money, success, and wealth. From notions of scarcity to self-doubt, we dissect the thoughts that sabotage financial endeavors, enabling readers to recognize and dismantle these mental roadblocks.

Reforming Belief Systems

Rewiring Thought Patterns:

Overcoming limiting beliefs is a transformative process of rewiring thought patterns. We delve into practical techniques that empower readers to challenge and reframe their beliefs. By replacing disempowering thoughts with empowering ones, individuals gain the mental tools needed to break free from the shackles of self-imposed limitations.

Affirmations and Positive Reinforcement:

Implementing affirmations as a powerful tool for reshaping belief systems. Through the strategic use of positive affirmations, readers learn to redirect their mental narratives and reinforce new, empowering beliefs. This section guides readers in creating personalized affirmations that align with their financial aspirations.

As readers progress through the process of overcoming limiting beliefs, the emphasis is not just on recognizing these constraints but on actively participating in their transformation. The goal is to empower individuals to become architects of their own beliefs, designing a mental landscape that fosters financial growth and abundance.

Practical Techniques for Transformation

Visualization for Belief Reinforcement:

Introducing the practice of visualization as a complementary technique to affirmations. By vividly imagining and emotionally connecting with a future where limiting beliefs no longer hold sway, readers cultivate a powerful mental environment that supports their financial goals.

Goal-Based Cognitive Restructuring:

Guiding readers through a goal-oriented approach to cognitive restructuring. By anchoring belief transformation to specific financial goals, individuals can systematically dismantle limiting beliefs that stand in the way of realizing their aspirations.

As readers emerge from this section, they carry with them not only the knowledge of how to identify and confront limiting beliefs but also the practical tools for transforming their mindset. Overcoming limiting beliefs becomes a dynamic process of self-empowerment, propelling individuals toward the threshold of the Millionaire Mindset with a renewed sense of belief and potential.

- Visualizing Financial Success

In the realm of the Millionaire Mindset, visualization is the magic wand that transforms dreams into tangible financial goals. This section navigates the process of visualizing financial success, providing readers with a powerful tool to shape their aspirations, enhance focus, and propel themselves toward the abundance they seek.

The Art of Visualization

Creating Vivid Mental Images:

Visualization begins with the creation of vivid mental images of financial success. Readers learn to harness their imagination to picture a future where their financial goals have been realized. This process involves not just seeing, but feeling the emotions associated with achieving those goals, creating a powerful and immersive experience within the mind.

Emotional Connection with Success:

Understanding the crucial role emotions play in visualization. Readers explore how to infuse their mental images with positive emotions, such as joy, satisfaction, and accomplishment. By forging an emotional connection with their financial success, individuals amplify the motivational impact of visualization.

Creating a Vision Board

Tangible Representations of Aspirations:

A vision board is a tangible manifestation of visualization. In this segment, readers discover the art of creating a vision board—a collage of images and affirmations that represent their financial goals. The process involves curating a visual representation of the desired lifestyle, assets, and achievements, serving as a daily reminder of what they are working towards.

Strategic Placement and Daily Reflection:

Guidance on strategically placing the vision board in prominent locations and incorporating it into daily routines. By making the vision board an integral part of their environment, readers continually reinforce their commitment to their financial aspirations, fostering a consistent and focused mindset.

The Transformative Impact

Visualizing Short-Term and Long-Term Goals:

Visualization is not limited to distant dreams but extends to short-term goals as well. Readers learn to adapt the practice to encompass both immediate financial milestones and long-term visions. This dual focus ensures that the benefits of visualization are felt throughout the entire financial journey.

Alignment with Action:

Highlighting the symbiotic relationship between visualization and action. Visualization serves as a motivational catalyst, inspiring individuals to take concrete steps toward their financial goals. Readers discover how to translate the energy generated through visualization into practical actions, creating a harmonious connection between mindset and behavior.

As readers immerse themselves in the process of visualizing financial success, they embark on a transformative journey that extends beyond wishful thinking. Visualization becomes a dynamic force, steering individuals toward the realization of their financial aspirations. By the end of this section, readers are equipped not only with the knowledge of how to visualize but also with a profound understanding of the impact visualization can have on their path to embracing the Millionaire Mindset.

- Cultivating Financial Confidence

In the symphony of financial success, confidence plays a pivotal role as the conductor, guiding decisions and actions towards prosperity. This section illuminates the process of cultivating financial confidence, empowering readers to navigate the complex landscape of wealth with assurance, resilience, and a can-do attitude.

Embracing Risk and Opportunity

Understanding the Paradox:

Financial success often involves a delicate balance between risk and opportunity. This segment explores the paradox of risk, helping readers understand that calculated risks are not liabilities but stepping stones towards growth. By dissecting common misconceptions around risk, readers develop a nuanced perspective that fosters confidence in making bold financial decisions.

Learning from Setbacks:

Confidence is forged in the crucible of setbacks. Readers are guided through the art of resilience, learning how to view failures not as roadblocks but as valuable lessons. By adopting a growth mindset, individuals cultivate the ability to bounce back from financial challenges with newfound wisdom and determination.

Building Resilience in the Face of Setbacks

The Power of Resilience:

Resilience is the cornerstone of financial confidence. This section delves into the psychology of resilience, equipping readers with strategies to bounce back from financial setbacks. By reframing setbacks as temporary hurdles rather than insurmountable obstacles, individuals build an enduring sense of confidence that withstands the trials of the financial journey.

Developing a Can-Do Attitude:

Confidence thrives in an environment of self-belief. Readers are guided through the process of developing a can-do attitude—an unwavering belief in one's ability to overcome challenges and achieve financial goals. By fostering a positive and proactive mindset, individuals cultivate the confidence needed to take decisive actions towards their financial aspirations.

Strategic Decision-Making

Strategies for Smart Decision-Making:

Confident decision-making is an art that can be cultivated. This segment provides practical strategies for making informed financial decisions. From conducting thorough research to seeking expert advice, readers gain the tools to approach decision-making with confidence, ensuring that each choice aligns with their financial goals.

Building Competency and Knowledge:

Confidence is intertwined with competency. Readers learn the importance of continuous learning and skill-building in the realm of finance. By expanding their financial knowledge and honing their skills, individuals enhance their confidence in making sound financial decisions, regardless of the complexity of the situation.

Cultivating financial confidence is not a one-time event but a dynamic process that evolves with experience and mindset. By the end of this section, readers are equipped not only with the understanding of the importance of confidence in financial success but also with actionable insights to nurture and sustain their financial confidence on the journey to embracing the Millionaire Mindset.

- Embracing Risk and Opportunity

In the pursuit of financial success, the ability to embrace risk and seize opportunities is a hallmark of the Millionaire Mindset. This section guides readers through the dynamic process of cultivating a mindset that not only acknowledges but welcomes risk as a catalyst for growth and views opportunities as stepping stones towards prosperity.

Understanding the Paradox

Calculation over Recklessness:

Embracing risk is not synonymous with recklessness; it's about calculated decision-making. This segment unpacks the paradox of risk, emphasizing the importance of assessing and understanding risks before taking action. By fostering a nuanced perspective on risk, readers learn to differentiate between strategic ventures and impulsive decisions.

Risk as a Growth Catalyst:

Risk, when managed effectively, becomes a powerful driver of growth. Readers explore how calculated risks, whether in investments, entrepreneurship, or career choices, can lead to substantial rewards. By reframing risk as an inherent part of the wealth-building journey, individuals begin to see it as an opportunity for expansion rather than a threat.

Learning from Setbacks

Resilience as a Confidence Builder:

Setbacks are an inevitable part of any financial journey. This section explores the concept that resilience in the face of setbacks is a key ingredient in embracing risk. Readers discover how each setback is a valuable lesson, contributing to the development of resilience and fortitude. By reframing failures as temporary setbacks, individuals build the confidence to navigate challenges.

Adopting a Growth Mindset:

A growth mindset is essential for embracing risk. Readers learn to view challenges not as insurmountable obstacles but as opportunities for learning and improvement. This mindset shift fosters a proactive approach to overcoming setbacks, contributing to a resilient and risk-embracing mindset.

Building Resilience in the Face of Setbacks

Psychology of Resilience:

Resilience is the bedrock of risk tolerance. This segment delves into the psychology of resilience, providing readers with tools to bounce back from setbacks. By understanding the cyclical nature of challenges and triumphs, individuals cultivate a mindset that views setbacks as temporary and surmountable, fostering the resilience needed to embrace future risks.

Learning from Failure:

Failure is not an end but a stepping stone towards success. Readers explore the narratives of successful individuals who have faced failures, learning how these experiences contributed to their eventual triumphs. By understanding that failure is not fatal but a part of the growth process, individuals build the resilience needed to embrace risks with confidence.

Embracing risk and opportunity is not about blind leaps of faith; it's a strategic and calculated process. By the end of this section, readers are equipped with the knowledge and mindset to navigate the delicate balance between risk and reward, laying the foundation for a financial journey guided by the principles of the Millionaire Mindset.

- Building Resilience in the Face of Setbacks

Resilience is the bedrock upon which the Millionaire Mindset is built. In this section, we embark on a transformative journey, exploring the process of building resilience in the face of setbacks. Readers will discover that setbacks are not roadblocks but growth opportunities, and resilience is the key to navigating the unpredictable terrain of the financial landscape.

The Power of Resilience

Understanding Resilience:

Resilience is the capacity to bounce back from adversity stronger than before. This section begins by defining resilience in the context of financial challenges. By understanding resilience as a dynamic and trainable quality, readers are encouraged to see setbacks as temporary detours rather than permanent roadblocks.

Overcoming the Fear of Failure:

A crucial aspect of resilience is overcoming the fear of failure. Readers explore the psychological aspects of failure, learning how to separate their self-worth from their financial setbacks. By reframing failure as a natural part of the learning process, individuals can diminish the fear associated with setbacks, allowing for a more resilient mindset.

Learning from Setbacks

Extracting Lessons from Adversity:

Setbacks, when approached with the right mindset, become invaluable lessons. This segment guides readers through the process of extracting lessons from financial challenges. By reflecting on the circumstances surrounding setbacks, individuals can identify patterns, refine strategies, and gain insights that contribute to future success.

The Growth Mindset Philosophy:

Building resilience involves adopting a growth mindset. Readers learn that setbacks are not permanent states but growth opportunities. By embracing a philosophy that views challenges as stepping stones toward improvement, individuals cultivate a mindset that not only endures setbacks but thrives on them.

Developing a Can-Do Attitude

Proactive Response to Adversity:

Resilience is not passive endurance but an active response to adversity. This section provides strategies for developing a can-do attitude—a mindset that seeks solutions and opportunities in the face of setbacks. By fostering a proactive response to challenges, individuals transform setbacks into catalysts for positive change.

Cultivating Emotional Strength:

Emotional strength is a cornerstone of resilience. Readers explore techniques for managing stress, anxiety, and negative emotions associated with setbacks. By developing emotional resilience, individuals can navigate financial challenges with clarity and composure, ensuring that emotions do not hinder their ability to rebound.

As readers progress through the process of building resilience in the face of setbacks, they emerge not only with the ability to endure financial challenges but with a mindset that thrives on adversity. By the end of this section, individuals are equipped to face setbacks with courage, learn from failures, and use each experience as a stepping stone towards the Millionaire Mindset.

- Developing a Can-Do Attitude

In the journey toward financial success, cultivating a can-do attitude is not just a mindset; it's a transformative force that propels individuals past challenges, turning setbacks into stepping stones. This section unravels the process of developing a can-do attitude—a mindset that embraces optimism, seeks solutions, and fosters resilience in the face of financial challenges.

Proactive Response to Adversity

Seeing Challenges as Opportunities:

A can-do attitude begins with viewing challenges not as insurmountable obstacles but as opportunities for growth and innovation. This section explores how a proactive mindset sees beyond setbacks, recognizing them as chances to learn, adapt, and ultimately thrive. By reframing adversity as a call to action, individuals set the stage for a can-do approach.

Solution-Oriented Thinking:

A can-do attitude is marked by a focus on solutions rather than dwelling on problems. Readers learn how to shift their mindset from dwelling on the negative aspects of a setback to actively seeking and implementing solutions. By cultivating solution-oriented thinking, individuals become architects of their success, regardless of the financial challenges they face.

Cultivating Emotional Strength

Managing Stress and Anxiety:

Emotional strength is a cornerstone of a can-do
attitude. This segment delves into practical
techniques for managing stress, anxiety, and
negative emotions that may arise during financial
challenges. By developing emotional resilience,
individuals can approach adversity with clarity and
composure, ensuring that emotions do not impede
their ability to respond effectively.

Maintaining Positivity Amidst Setbacks:

A can-do attitude thrives on positivity, even amid
setbacks. Readers explore strategies for maintaining
a positive outlook and fostering resilience during
challenging times. By consciously cultivating
optimism, individuals not only navigate financial
challenges more effectively but also contribute to a
mindset that attracts positive outcomes.

Cultivating Emotional Strength

Turning Setbacks into Stepping Stones

Learning and Growing from Setbacks:

A can-do attitude transforms setbacks into opportunities for learning and growth. Readers discover the importance of extracting lessons from financial challenges and applying them to future endeavors. By adopting a growth mindset, individuals view setbacks not as failures but as integral steps on the path to success.

Adopting a Forward-Thinking Perspective:

A can-do attitude is forward-thinking and focused on the possibilities that lie ahead. This section guides readers to develop a forward-looking perspective, emphasizing the importance of setting new goals, adapting strategies, and maintaining momentum even in the face of setbacks. By staying future-oriented, individuals embody the essence of a can-do attitude.

As readers immerse themselves in the process of developing a can-do attitude, they undergo a profound transformation. By the end of this section, individuals are not only equipped with practical tools for proactive problem-solving and emotional resilience but are infused with a mindset that not only endures challenges but actively embraces them as opportunities for growth and success on the journey to the Millionaire Mindset.

CHAPTER 2: CRAFTING YOUR FINANCIAL BLUEPRINT

Welcome to the blueprinting phase of your financial journey—an exhilarating chapter that invites you to be the architect of your financial destiny. In "Crafting Your Financial Blueprint," we transition from the theoretical realm of mindset to the practical terrain of planning. Just as a skilled architect meticulously plans the construction of a masterpiece, you are about to embark on the meticulous design of your financial future.

In the previous chapter, we unveiled the secrets of the Millionaire Mindset, laying the foundation for a mindset rooted in positivity, resilience, and a proactive approach to challenges. Now, armed with this transformative mindset, it's time to channel your aspirations into a tangible and personalized financial plan—a blueprint that will guide you through the intricate pathways of wealth creation and financial fulfilment.

Setting SMART Financial Goals

Defining the Landscape of Your Dreams:

Crafting Your Financial Blueprint begins with setting SMART goals—Specific, Measurable, Achievable, Relevant, and Time-bound. In this section, we will explore the art of articulating your financial dreams in clear and concrete terms. Whether it's homeownership, world travel, or early retirement, your goals will become the North Star guiding your financial decisions and actions.

Aligning Goals with Your Values:

Your financial goals are not just about numbers; they are a reflection of your values and priorities. We'll delve into the process of aligning your financial aspirations with your core values, ensuring that your journey to prosperity is not only lucrative but also deeply fulfilling on a personal level.

Creating a Personalized Financial Plan

From Dreams to Reality:

With your goals in focus, we move on to the practical steps of creating a personalized financial plan. From budgeting and saving strategies to emergency funds and investment planning, you will learn how to translate your aspirations into actionable steps. This section is the bridge between the dreams you've envisioned and the concrete actions that will turn them into reality.

Mapping Short-Term and Long-Term Strategies:

Your financial journey is a dynamic expedition with both short-term milestones and long-term objectives. We will explore the importance of balancing immediate financial needs with strategic, forward-thinking plans. Crafting a financial blueprint involves not only reaching your goals today but also building the foundation for the wealth you envision in the years to come.

As you navigate through the chapters of Crafting Your Financial Blueprint, envision yourself as the architect of a grand structure—your financial future. Your goals, aspirations, and values will be the building blocks, and this blueprint will be your guide. Let's embark on this journey together, shaping a future where financial prosperity is not just a vision but a meticulously planned reality waiting to unfold.

- Setting SMART Financial Goals

Setting financial goals is not merely a wishful exercise but a strategic process that forms the cornerstone of your financial blueprint. In this section, we delve into the intricacies of crafting SMART financial goals—goals that are Specific, Measurable, Achievable, Relevant, and Time-bound. This process empowers you to transform your aspirations into a concrete roadmap for financial success.

Defining the Landscape of Your Dreams

Specificity:

The journey begins with the art of specificity. Rather than vague desires, SMART financial goals demand clarity. What do you aspire to achieve? Be it buying a home, clearing debts, or building a robust investment portfolio, specificity provides a clear target, enabling focused efforts and strategic planning.

Measurability:

Measurable goals allow you to track progress and celebrate milestones. We explore the importance of quantifying your financial objectives. Whether in terms of savings, investments, or debt reduction, establishing measurable criteria provides tangible benchmarks, ensuring you stay on course toward your financial destination.

Aligning Goals with Your Values

Achievability:

While ambition is encouraged, goals must also be achievable. This section guides you through the process of setting targets that are challenging yet realistic. By considering your current financial situation, resources, and capabilities, you ensure that your goals are within reach, fostering a sense of accomplishment as you attain them.

Relevance:

Aligning financial goals with your values is crucial for sustained motivation. We explore the relevance of your aspirations to your life's purpose and principles. When goals resonate with your core values, the pursuit becomes not just a financial journey but a meaningful and fulfilling endeavor.

Mapping Short-Term and Long-Term Strategies

Time-bound:

The ticking clock introduces a sense of urgency. We discuss the significance of establishing time frames for your goals. Whether short-term objectives or long-term visions, assigning deadlines creates a sense of accountability and prompts strategic planning. It transforms aspirations into a timeline, propelling you toward consistent and focused action.

Balancing Immediate Needs with Future Plans:

Financial success is a dynamic interplay between the present and the future. We guide you through the delicate balance of addressing immediate financial needs while strategically planning for the long term. Crafting a financial blueprint involves not only reaching goals today but also building a foundation for sustained prosperity.

As you navigate the process of setting SMART financial goals, envision yourself not just as a goal-setter but as a strategic architect shaping the contours of your financial destiny. This section empowers you to articulate your dreams with precision, ensuring that every financial goal becomes a stepping stone toward the realization of your grand vision for the future.

- Defining Short-Term and Long-Term Objectives

In the intricate process of crafting your financial blueprint, the distinction between short-term and long-term objectives is a compass that guides your financial journey. This section illuminates the strategic process of defining short-term and long-term objectives—two pillars that, when harmonized, provide a balanced foundation for sustained financial success.

The Dynamics of Short-Term Objectives

Immediacy and Tangibility:

Short-term objectives are the immediate building blocks of your financial blueprint. They encompass goals achievable within the next one to three years. This section encourages you to identify objectives with a sense of immediacy and tangibility—financial milestones that you can reach shortly. Whether it's building an emergency fund, paying off high-interest debts, or saving for a specific expense, short-term objectives inject momentum into your financial journey.

Adaptability and Flexibility:

In the realm of short-term objectives, adaptability is key. Life is dynamic, and financial circumstances can change rapidly. We explore the importance of flexibility in adjusting short-term goals based on evolving situations. This adaptability ensures that your financial blueprint remains responsive to real-time challenges and opportunities.

The Vision of Long-Term Goals

Strategic Horizon:

Long-term objectives extend your financial vision beyond the immediate horizon. Covering a period of three or more years, these goals involve more profound financial aspirations. This section guides you in envisioning your financial future—be it saving for a home, funding education, or building a retirement nest egg. Long-term goals provide the framework for sustained financial stability and growth.

Consistency and Patience:

Achieving long-term objectives requires consistency and patience. We explore the discipline needed to adhere to a strategic plan over an extended period. This involves making deliberate choices today that align with the vision you have for the future. Long-term goals are a testament to your commitment to enduring financial success.

Balancing Immediate Needs with Strategic Vision

Integration of Short-Term and Long-Term Planning:

The magic of crafting your financial blueprint lies in the harmonious integration of short-term and long-term planning. This section provides insights into striking the right balance between addressing immediate financial needs and strategically planning for the future. It's a delicate dance that ensures you not only meet pressing obligations but also build a foundation for sustained prosperity.

Reviewing and Adjusting Goals:

The financial landscape is ever-evolving, and your goals should evolve with it. Regular review and adjustment of both short-term and long-term objectives are essential. We discuss how periodic evaluations enable you to align your goals with changing circumstances, ensuring that your financial blueprint remains a dynamic and effective guide.

As you navigate the process of defining short-term and long-term objectives, envision yourself as an architect meticulously planning a structure that stands the test of time. Your short-term goals lay the foundation, while your long-term aspirations shape the grandeur of the edifice. Together, they form the blueprint for a future where financial success is both immediate and enduring.

- Aligning Goals with Personal Values

In the intricate process of crafting your financial blueprint, aligning your goals with personal values is the compass that ensures your journey is not just financially prosperous but deeply meaningful and fulfilling. This section delves into the transformative process of connecting your financial aspirations with the core values that define who you are.

Unveiling Core Values

Identifying What Matters Most:

Aligning goals with personal values begins with a deep exploration of your core beliefs and priorities. This section encourages introspection to identify what truly matters most to you. Whether it's family, education, community impact, or personal growth, understanding your values forms the bedrock of meaningful financial goal-setting.

Prioritizing Values:

Not all values are created equal. We explore the art of prioritizing values to ensure that your financial goals are in harmony with the aspects of life that hold the utmost significance for you. This prioritization process guides you in making choices that resonate with your deepest convictions.

Crafting Meaningful Financial Goals

Connecting Aspirations to Values:

Financial goals cease to be mere numbers; they become vehicles for expressing and enhancing your values. This section guides you in translating your aspirations into concrete financial objectives that directly align with your core values. Whether it's philanthropy, education for your children, or sustainable living, your goals become a reflection of your values in action.

Evaluating Trade-Offs and Choices:

Aligning goals with personal values involves making intentional choices. We discuss the concept of trade-offs—understanding that every financial decision involves giving up something to gain something else. By evaluating trade-offs through the lens of your values, you ensure that your financial choices contribute to the life you want to lead.

Ensuring Meaningful Financial Success

Sustainable and Fulfilling Prosperity:

The alignment of goals and values isn't just about achieving financial success; it's about sustaining and finding fulfilment in that success. This section explores the concept of sustainable prosperity, where financial achievements are not only lucrative but contribute to a life rich in purpose and satisfaction.

Measuring Success beyond Numbers:

Success is measured not only in monetary terms but also in the fulfilment of your values. We guide you in developing metrics that go beyond financial indicators, allowing you to gauge success based on the alignment of your actions with your values. This holistic approach ensures that your financial journey is a true reflection of the life you aspire to lead.

As you engage in the process of aligning your goals with personal values, envision yourself not just as a financial planner but as a curator of a life rich in meaning. Your financial blueprint becomes a tapestry woven with the threads of your values, creating a future where success is not just measured in wealth but in the alignment of your financial journey with the essence of who you are.

- Establishing Measurable Milestones

In the intricate tapestry of financial success, measurable milestones act as the threads that weave your aspirations into a tangible reality. This section navigates the strategic process of establishing measurable milestones—quantifiable checkpoints that not only mark progress but also serve as guideposts on your journey toward financial prosperity.

Clarifying the Path Forward

Breaking Down Goals into Tangible Steps:

Establishing measurable milestones begins with breaking down your overarching financial goals into manageable and quantifiable steps. This section guides you in deconstructing larger aspirations into smaller, achievable components. By doing so, you gain clarity on the specific actions required to propel you toward your ultimate objectives.

Quantifying Progress:

Measurable milestones serve as metrics for progress. We delve into the importance of quantifying your journey—whether in terms of savings, debt reduction, or investment growth. This quantification not only provides a clear picture of how far you've come but also fuels motivation by highlighting achievements along the way.

Aligning with Time-Bound Objectives

Integration with Time Frames:

Measurable milestones find their significance within the context of time-bound objectives. This section explores the dynamic relationship between timelines and milestones. By aligning measurable achievements with specific time frames, you create a structured and goal-oriented roadmap, ensuring that progress remains steady and consistent.

Ensuring Accountability and Focus:

Measurable milestones serve as checkpoints that demand accountability. We discuss how these quantifiable steps enhance focus by providing tangible targets. Regularly measuring progress against these milestones not only holds you accountable but also reinforces a sense of purpose, keeping your financial journey on track.

Celebrating Achievements and Adjusting Course

Recognition of Accomplishments:

Each measurable milestone achieved is a cause for celebration. This section emphasizes the importance of acknowledging and celebrating your financial victories, no matter how small. Recognizing accomplishments not only boosts morale but also reinforces the positive habits and behaviors that contribute to your overall financial success.

Flexibility for Adjustments:

The financial journey is dynamic, and adjustments are sometimes necessary. We explore the concept of flexibility in the face of changing circumstances. Measurable milestones are not rigid; they can be adjusted to align with evolving goals, ensuring that your financial blueprint remains adaptable to the twists and turns of life.

The Synergy of Progress and Motivation

Motivation as a Result of Progress:

Measurable milestones create a powerful feedback loop with motivation. This section elucidates how the act of achieving quantifiable steps fuels motivation, propelling you forward with renewed energy and determination. The synergy between progress and motivation transforms your financial journey into a dynamic and fulfilling endeavor.

Strategic Planning for Ongoing Success:

As you establish measurable milestones, envision yourself not just reaching specific financial targets but strategically planning for ongoing success. Each milestone becomes a building block, contributing to the solid foundation of your financial blueprint. By the end of this section, you will not only be equipped with measurable markers for success but also infused with the motivation to reach them, ensuring that your financial journey is both intentional and rewarding.

- Creating a Personalized Financial Plan

In the symphony of financial success, a personalized financial plan is a conductor that harmonizes your aspirations with strategic actions. This section illuminates the process of creating a personalized financial plan—a comprehensive roadmap tailored to your unique goals, values, and circumstances.

Navigating Your Financial Landscape

Assessment of Current Financial Situation:

The journey begins with a thorough assessment of your current financial landscape. This section guides you in taking stock of your income, expenses, debts, and assets. Understanding where you stand financially is the compass that directs your financial plan toward realistic and achievable goals.

Identifying Short-Term and Long-Term Objectives:

Your financial plan is a compass, and your objectives are the destinations. We delve into the process of identifying both short-term and long-term financial objectives. By aligning your immediate needs with your future aspirations, your plan takes on a dynamic structure that accommodates the ebb and flow of life.

Translating Goals into Actionable Steps

Budgeting and Expense Management:

A personalized financial plan involves translating your goals into actionable steps. We explore the art of budgeting, providing practical insights into managing your income and expenses. By allocating resources strategically, you pave the way for achieving your financial milestones.

Emergency Funds and Risk Management:

Life is unpredictable, and a robust financial plan incorporates provisions for unforeseen events. This section delves into the importance of emergency funds and risk management. By establishing a financial safety net, you fortify your plan against unexpected challenges, ensuring that setbacks don't derail your progress.

Strategic Savings and Investment Strategies

Building Savings for Short-Term Goals:

Savings are the fuel that propels your financial journey. This segment provides strategies for building savings tailored to your short-term objectives. Whether it's for a vacation, a home purchase, or starting a business, strategic savings become the catalysts for turning dreams into reality.

Investment Planning for Long-Term Growth:

Long-term goals require the power of compounding and growth. We delve into the realm of investment planning, guiding you through the process of building a portfolio aligned with your risk tolerance and long-term objectives. By harnessing the potential of investments, your plan becomes a vehicle for sustained wealth creation.

Periodic Review and Adaptation

Continuous Monitoring and Adjustments:

A personalized financial plan is not static; it's a dynamic framework that evolves with your life. This section emphasizes the importance of continuous monitoring and adjustments. Regular reviews ensure that your plan remains aligned with changing circumstances, allowing you to adapt proactively to new opportunities and challenges.

Professional Guidance and Expert Advice:

In the creation of a personalized financial plan, seeking professional guidance can be invaluable. We discuss the role of financial advisors and experts in fine-tuning your plan, and providing insights and strategies that enhance its effectiveness.

As you embark on the process of creating your personalized financial plan, envision yourself not merely as a planner but as a visionary architect shaping the blueprint for your financial future. By the end of this section, your plan will not only be a reflection of your goals and values but a powerful instrument guiding you toward the realization of your aspirations.

- Budgeting Basics: From Essentials to Luxuries

In the pursuit of financial wellness, the cornerstone is a well-crafted budget that aligns your spending with your goals and priorities. This section illuminates the budgeting basics, guiding you from distinguishing essentials to navigating the realm of luxuries, ensuring that every dollar spent is a deliberate choice contributing to your overall financial well-being.

Defining Essentials

Basic Needs and Living Expenses:

Budgeting begins with a clear delineation of essentials. We explore the fundamental elements that constitute your basic needs—housing, utilities, groceries, transportation, and healthcare. By prioritizing these essentials, you establish a solid foundation for financial stability.

Fixed vs. Variable Expenses:

Within essentials, understanding the distinction between fixed and variable expenses is crucial. This section delves into the concept of fixed expenses, such as rent or mortgage, which remain constant, and variable expenses, such as groceries or utilities, which may fluctuate. This understanding enables you to allocate your resources effectively.

Navigating Non-Essential Spending

Discretionary Spending:

Once essentials are addressed, attention turns to discretionary spending—the realm of non-essential expenses. We guide you through the process of categorizing discretionary spending, including entertainment, dining out, and luxury items. This distinction empowers you to make intentional choices that align with your financial goals.

Setting Spending Priorities:

Not all non-essential spending is created equal. This section explores the art of setting priorities within discretionary spending. By identifying what brings you joy and aligns with your values, you can allocate resources to the areas that matter most, ensuring that non-essential spending is both enjoyable and purposeful.

The Role of Savings in Budgeting

Allocating for Savings:

A robust budget doesn't just allocate for spending—it prioritizes savings. We discuss the importance of earmarking a portion of your income for savings, including emergency funds, short-term goals, and long-term investments. Savings become the seeds for future financial growth and security.

Emergency Funds and Future Planning:

Within savings, establishing emergency funds is paramount. This section delves into the purpose and importance of emergency funds as a financial safety net. Additionally, we explore how savings contribute to future planning, ensuring that your budget is not just about the present but also about building a foundation for future financial success.

Balancing Enjoyment and Financial Goals

Mindful Spending on Luxuries:

Luxuries add enjoyment to life, but budgeting requires mindfulness in their allocation. We discuss strategies for incorporating luxuries into your budget without jeopardizing your financial goals. By striking a balance between enjoyment and financial responsibility, you can indulge in luxuries without compromising your overall financial well-being.

Periodic Review and Adjustment:

Budgeting is not a one-time activity but a dynamic process. This section emphasizes the importance of periodic review and adjustment. Life evolves, and so should your budget. Regular assessments ensure that your budget remains aligned with your goals, allowing for adaptability to changing circumstances.

As you delve into the intricacies of budgeting basics—from essentials to luxuries—envision yourself not just as a financial planner but as a mindful curator of your financial well-being. By the end of this section, you will have the tools to craft a budget that not only meets your basic needs but also enhances your quality of life and propels you toward your broader financial goals.

- Building an Emergency Fund

In the orchestra of financial wellness, an emergency fund plays a pivotal role as the safety net that shields you from unexpected storms. This section illuminates the strategic process of building an emergency fund—a financial cushion that provides stability and peace of mind in the face of unforeseen challenges.

Understanding the Importance of an Emergency Fund

Financial Resilience in Uncertain Times:

An emergency fund is your financial fortress, providing a buffer against the uncertainties of life. We delve into the importance of financial resilience and how an emergency fund acts as a shield, allowing you to weather unexpected expenses, job loss, or medical emergencies without jeopardizing your overall financial stability.

Breaking the Cycle of Debt:

One of the primary roles of an emergency fund is to break the cycle of debt. This section explores how having a financial cushion reduces the reliance on credit cards or loans to address emergencies. By avoiding debt, you maintain financial control and prevent interest payments from eroding your long-term financial goals.

Determining the Right Size for Your Emergency Fund

Calculating Basic Living Expenses:

Building an emergency fund begins with understanding your basic living expenses. We guide you through the process of calculating the essential costs of housing, utilities, groceries, transportation, and healthcare. This forms the foundation for determining the size of your emergency fund.

Assessing Individual Risk Factors:

Not all emergencies are created equal. This section explores individual risk factors, such as job stability, health considerations, and lifestyle that influence the size of your emergency fund. By tailoring your fund to your unique circumstances, you ensure it is robust enough to handle your specific challenges.

Establishing a Systematic Savings Plan

Setting Realistic Savings Goals:

Building an emergency fund involves setting realistic savings goals. We discuss strategies for determining an achievable target based on your monthly living expenses and individual risk factors. By breaking down the goal into manageable increments, you make the process more attainable.

Automating Savings Contributions:

Consistency is key in building an emergency fund. This section explores the benefits of automating your savings contributions. By setting up automatic transfers, you ensure a regular and disciplined approach to building your fund, turning saving into a habit rather than a sporadic activity.

Making Strategic Use of Windfalls

Allocating Windfalls to Your Fund:

Windfalls, such as tax refunds or bonuses, provide an opportunity to boost your emergency fund. We discuss the strategic allocation of unexpected financial gains to accelerate the growth of your fund. By making intentional choices with windfalls, you expedite the process of achieving your savings goals.

Reassessing and Adjusting Over Time:

As life evolves, so do your financial needs. This section emphasizes the importance of reassessing and adjusting your emergency fund over time. Changes in income, expenses, or risk factors may necessitate modifications to the size of your fund. Regular reviews ensure that your emergency fund remains aligned with your current circumstances.

Celebrating Financial Preparedness

Peace of Mind and Financial Freedom:

Building an emergency fund is not just about the numbers; it's about peace of mind and financial freedom. We discuss the emotional and psychological benefits of knowing you have a financial safety net. By celebrating each milestone in the growth of your emergency fund, you reinforce the positive habits contributing to your overall financial well-being.

Transitioning to Future Financial Goals:

Once your emergency fund reaches its target, you transition from building to maintaining. This section explores how a well-established emergency fund allows you to redirect your focus and resources toward future financial goals, such as debt reduction, investments, or saving for specific aspirations.

As you engage in the process of building an emergency fund, envision yourself not just as a saver but as a guardian of your financial security. By the end of this section, you will have fortified your financial foundation, equipped with an emergency fund that empowers you to face uncertainties with confidence and ensures that your financial journey is built on a solid and resilient footing.

- Planning for Major Expenses and Investments

In the pursuit of financial wellness, thoughtful planning for major expenses and investments becomes the compass that guides your financial journey. This section illuminates the strategic process of planning for significant financial outlays—whether it's a major purchase, education, or investment—ensuring that each decision aligns with your broader financial goals.

Identifying Major Expenses and Investments

Defining Financial Milestones:

Planning begins with a clear identification of major expenses and investments. We explore how life's financial milestones, such as buying a home, funding education, or starting a business, become pivotal points on your financial roadmap. By recognizing these milestones, you can strategically plan for their financial implications.

Distinguishing Between Short-Term and Long-Term Goals:

Major expenses and investments can span various timeframes. This section delves into the distinction between short-term and long-term goals. Whether it's a vacation shortly or retirement decades away, understanding the temporal aspects of your goals informs the planning process.

Estimating Costs and Setting Realistic Goals

Researching and Estimating Costs:

Accurate planning requires a realistic estimate of the costs involved. We discuss the importance of thorough research in understanding the financial implications of your goals. Whether it's the price of a home, tuition fees, or the capital required for an investment, precise estimates lay the foundation for effective planning.

Setting Achievable Savings Targets:

Major expenses and investments often involve a substantial financial commitment. This section guides you in setting achievable savings targets. By breaking down the total cost into manageable increments and establishing a timeline, you create a systematic savings plan that aligns with your goals.

Exploring Financing Options and Investment Strategies

Understanding Financing Options:

For major expenses like a home or education, financing may be necessary. We explore the various financing options available, such as mortgages, loans, or education funding. Understanding the implications of each option empowers you to make informed decisions that complement your overall financial strategy.

Strategizing Investment Approaches:

Investments play a crucial role in planning for long-term goals. This section delves into strategic investment approaches tailored to your objectives. Whether it's building a diversified portfolio for retirement or exploring specific investment vehicles for shorter-term goals, a thoughtful investment strategy enhances the potential for financial success.

Integrating Major Expenses with Overall Financial Goals

Aligning with Your Financial Blueprint:

Major expenses and investments are not isolated events; they are integral components of your overall financial plan. We discuss the importance of aligning these financial decisions with the broader context of your financial blueprint. Each major expense becomes a deliberate step forward on your journey toward financial wellness.

Ensuring Flexibility and Adaptability:

Life is dynamic, and plans may need adjustment. This section emphasizes the need for flexibility in your planning. Whether it's adapting to changes in income, adjusting timelines, or reevaluating investment strategies, flexibility ensures that your financial plan remains resilient in the face of evolving circumstances.

Celebrating Achievements and Progress Milestones as Markers of Success:

Each major expense or investment marks a significant milestone in your financial journey. This section encourages you to celebrate these achievements, recognizing them as markers of success. By acknowledging your progress, you reinforce positive financial habits and motivate yourself to continue moving toward your broader goals.

As you successfully plan for and achieve major expenses and investments, you transition to the next chapter of your financial journey. This could involve setting new goals, reassessing priorities, or redirecting resources toward different aspirations. Planning becomes a dynamic and ongoing process, ensuring that your financial wellness evolves with you.

As you engage in the process of planning for major expenses and investments, envision yourself not just as a planner but as the architect of your financial future. By the end of this section, you will have navigated the complexities of major financial decisions, fortified your financial foundation, and positioned yourself to achieve the milestones that contribute to your overall financial wellness.

CHAPTER 3:
MASTERING THE ART OF BUDGETING AND SAVING

Welcome to the Heart of Financial Mastery—a chapter dedicated to the art of budgeting and saving. In the symphony of financial well-being, your ability to craft and adhere to a budget, coupled with the discipline of strategic saving, forms the cornerstone of your financial masterpiece. As we delve into this chapter, imagine yourself not as a passive observer but as a skilled sculptor, molding and shaping your financial future with purpose and precision.

Unveiling the Power of Budgeting

Budgeting as Your Financial Canvas:

Budgeting is not a restraint but a canvas upon which you paint the picture of your financial success. This section explores the transformative power of budgeting, allowing you to allocate resources intentionally, make informed financial decisions, and, most importantly, direct your money toward the achievement of your goals.

From Essentials to Luxuries:

Budgeting is a journey from essentials to luxuries, and every dollar you allocate is a brushstroke on your financial canvas. We unravel the dynamics of categorizing expenses, distinguishing between needs and wants, and finding the delicate balance that ensures both financial responsibility and the enjoyment of life.

The Strategic Art of Saving

Saving as the Sculptor's Chisel:

Saving is the sculptor's chisel, carving out the intricate details of your financial sculpture. We delve into the strategic art of saving, guiding you to build a robust financial foundation. From emergency funds to strategic savings for goals and investments, each saving strategy contributes to the resilience and beauty of your financial masterpiece.

Automating Success:

The art of saving extends beyond intention—it thrives on consistency. This section explores the concept of automating your savings, turning the act of saving into a habit rather than a conscious decision. By automating your financial contributions, you ensure that your masterpiece takes shape steadily and systematically.

 Crafting Your Financial Vision

Budgeting and Saving as Creative Expression:

Your budget and savings plan are not just financial tools; they are expressions of your creativity and vision. We discuss how crafting a budget and saving strategically enable you to manifest your financial aspirations. Your financial masterpiece is a reflection of the life you envision, shaped by your deliberate choices and actions.

Balancing Immediate Gratification and Future Goals:

Budgeting and saving require a delicate balance between immediate gratification and future goals. This section explores the art of making choices that honor both present enjoyment and future aspirations. By finding equilibrium, you ensure that your financial masterpiece is not only financially sound but also a source of fulfilment and joy.

Navigating Challenges and Celebrating Success

Overcoming Obstacles:

Every artist faces challenges, and the financial sculptor is no different. We discuss common challenges in budgeting and saving and provide strategies for overcoming them. From unexpected expenses to fluctuating income, you'll learn to adapt and refine your masterpiece in the face of challenges.

Celebrating Milestones:

In the journey of financial mastery, every milestone is a cause for celebration. This section encourages you to celebrate the completion of a successful budget, the achievement of savings goals, and the progress made toward your financial vision. By recognizing and commemorating these milestones, you infuse your financial journey with a sense of achievement and motivation.

As you embark on the exploration of mastering the art of budgeting and saving, envision yourself not only as a financial planner but as an artist shaping a masterpiece that transcends numbers. By the end of this chapter, you'll not only have honed the skills of budgeting and saving but will have sculpted a financial masterpiece that reflects your vision, values, and the life you aspire to lead.

- Budgeting for a Life of Abundance

In the canvas of your financial journey, the art of budgeting takes on a new dimension when viewed through the lens of abundance. This section invites you to shift your perspective from scarcity to abundance, transforming budgeting into a tool for not just financial stability but for cultivating a life rich in fulfilment and prosperity.

The Abundance Mindset

Shifting Perspectives:

Budgeting for a life of abundance begins with a fundamental shift in perspective. We explore the concept of the abundance mindset—a mindset that sees opportunities instead of obstacles, celebrates progress rather than dwelling on limitations, and views budgeting not as a restriction but as a means to unlock possibilities.

Embracing Gratitude:

Central to the abundance mindset is the practice of gratitude. This section delves into the transformative power of gratitude in budgeting. By appreciating the resources you have and expressing gratitude for financial blessings, you cultivate a positive relationship with your finances, setting the stage for abundance to flourish.

Crafting an Abundant Budget

Aligning Spending with Values:

An abundant budget is not just about numbers; it's about aligning your spending with your values and priorities. We guide you in crafting a budget that reflects what truly matters to you. By directing resources toward experiences, relationships, and personal growth, your budget becomes a tool for creating a life of abundance.

Investing in Personal Growth:

Budgeting for a life of abundance extends beyond immediate needs. We explore the art of allocating resources for personal growth and development.

Whether it's investing in education, skills, or experiences that enrich your life, your budget becomes a vehicle for continuous personal expansion.

The Joy of Strategic Saving

Savings as Seeds of Abundance:

Saving takes on a new dimension when seen as planting seeds of abundance. This section explores strategic saving not just for emergencies but for creating opportunities and realizing dreams. By nurturing your savings with intention, you cultivate a garden of financial abundance that yields a bountiful harvest over time.

Emergency Fund as a Source of Security:

Even in the realm of abundance, the emergency fund remains a cornerstone. We discuss how an abundant mindset enhances the purpose of an emergency fund, transforming it from a safety net to a source of security that allows you to navigate life's uncertainties with confidence.

Embracing Enjoyment and Generosity

Balancing Enjoyment and Financial Goals:

Budgeting for abundance involves striking a harmonious balance between enjoyment and financial goals. We explore strategies for incorporating moments of joy and fulfilment into your budget. Whether it's travel, hobbies, or other sources of happiness, your budget becomes a tool for intentional enjoyment.

Cultivating Generosity:

An abundant life includes the joy of giving. This section delves into the transformative power of generosity in budgeting. By allocating resources for charitable contributions or acts of kindness, you not only contribute to the well-being of others but also invite a sense of abundance into your own life.

Nurturing Abundance Amid Challenges

Navigating Financial Challenges with Grace:

Even in an abundant life, challenges may arise. We discuss how maintaining an abundance mindset can guide you through financial difficulties with grace and resilience. By reframing challenges as opportunities for growth, you continue to nurture a life of abundance even in the face of adversity.

Celebrating Every Financial Victory:

In the journey of abundance, every financial victory, no matter how small, is worthy of celebration. This section encourages you to acknowledge and savor each milestone in your budgeting journey. By celebrating successes, you amplify the positive energy that propels you toward a life filled with abundance.

As you explore the art of budgeting for a life of abundance, envision yourself not just as a budgeter but as a creator of a masterpiece—a life rich in joy, fulfilment, and prosperity. By the end of this section, you will have not only mastered the practical aspects of budgeting but will have infused your financial journey with the transformative energy of abundance.

- Creating a Realistic and Sustainable Budget

In the intricate dance of financial mastery, creating a realistic and sustainable budget is akin to composing a symphony that harmonizes your financial goals with the rhythms of your everyday life. This section delves into the strategic process of crafting a budget that not only reflects your aspirations but is also resilient in the face of life's ever-changing cadence.

Understanding Your Financial Landscape

Assessment of Income and Expenses:

Creating a realistic budget begins with a comprehensive assessment of your financial landscape. We guide you through the process of understanding your income streams, distinguishing between fixed and variable expenses, and gaining clarity on your financial inflows and outflows.

Honesty and Transparency:

A sustainable budget thrives on honesty and transparency. This section explores the importance of being candid about your financial habits, needs, and desires. By facing your financial reality head-on, you lay the foundation for a budget that reflects your true circumstances and paves the way for meaningful financial decisions.

Identifying Needs and Wants

Distinguishing Between Essentials and Discretionary Spending:

A realistic budget hinges on the ability to distinguish between needs and wants. We delve into the process of categorizing expenses into essentials and discretionary spending. This distinction becomes the guiding principle that ensures your budget addresses immediate needs while allowing room for intentional enjoyment.

Prioritization for Sustainability:

Sustainability lies in prioritization. This section guides you in prioritizing your spending based on necessities, values, and long-term goals. By aligning your budget with your priorities, you create a sustainable financial plan that withstands the test of time.

Setting Achievable Goals

Strategic Goal-Setting:

Goals are the compass that guides your budgeting journey. We discuss the art of setting achievable and realistic financial goals. By breaking down larger objectives into manageable milestones, you transform your aspirations into actionable steps, ensuring that your budget becomes a roadmap for success.

Timeline and Phasing:

Sustainability also involves considering the timeline for your goals. This section explores the concept of phasing—aligning your goals with specific timeframes and life stages. By adapting your budget to the evolving nature of your aspirations, you ensure that it remains relevant and effective.

Allocating for Savings and Emergencies

Prioritizing Savings Contributions:

Savings are the pillars of financial sustainability. We guide you in allocating a portion of your income to savings with intention and consistency. Whether it's for short-term goals, long-term investments, or emergency funds, strategic savings contributions fortify the resilience of your budget.

Emergency Funds as a Financial Safety Net:

A sustainable budget acknowledges the unpredictable nature of life. This section explores the critical role of emergency funds as a financial safety net. By incorporating provisions for unforeseen circumstances, your budget becomes adaptive and capable of weathering unexpected challenges.

Embracing Flexibility and Adaptability

Flexible Budget Categories:

Life is dynamic, and a sustainable budget is flexible. We discuss the importance of building flexibility into your budget categories. Whether it's adjusting discretionary spending or adapting to changing income, a flexible budget accommodates the fluidity of life.

Regular Reviews and Adjustments:

Sustainability involves regular check-ins and adjustments. This section emphasizes the significance of periodic reviews of your budget. By staying attuned to changes in your financial landscape, you empower yourself to make informed adjustments, ensuring that your budget remains an effective tool for financial mastery.

Celebrating Progress and Reinforcing Habits

Acknowledging Financial Wins:

In the journey of creating a realistic and sustainable budget, every financial win is a cause for celebration. This section encourages you to acknowledge and celebrate your progress. By recognizing your achievements, you reinforce positive financial habits and motivation to stay on course.

Continuous Learning and Improvement:

A sustainable budget is a work in progress. We discuss the concept of continuous learning and improvement. By adopting a mindset of growth and adaptability, you position yourself to refine and enhance your budgeting skills over time, ensuring that your financial mastery evolves with you.

As you engage in the process of creating a realistic and sustainable budget, envision yourself not just as a budgeter but as a composer orchestrating a symphony of financial success. By the end of this section, you will not only have crafted a budget that aligns with your aspirations but will have laid the groundwork for a sustainable financial journey that endures and thrives.

- Strategies for Smart Spending

In the canvas of financial mastery, smart spending emerges as the brushstroke that transforms your budget into a masterpiece of financial success. This section unveils a spectrum of strategies aimed at elevating your spending habits from mere transactions to intentional choices that align with your goals, values, and the pursuit of a financially fulfilling life.

Cultivating Mindful Consumption

Conscious Spending Habits:

Smart spending begins with cultivating mindful consumption habits. We explore the concept of conscious spending—making choices that align with your values and contribute to your overall well-being. By bringing awareness to your purchasing decisions, you transform spending into a deliberate and purposeful act.

Needs vs. Wants Evaluation:

A fundamental aspect of mindful consumption is the evaluation of needs versus wants. This section guides you through the process of discerning between essential purchases and discretionary spending. By consciously addressing your needs first, you ensure that your budget serves as a tool for sustainable and intentional financial choices.

Utilizing Technology and Tools

Budgeting Apps and Expense Tracking:

Technology becomes your ally in the journey of smart spending. We discuss the benefits of budgeting apps and expense-tracking tools. By leveraging these resources, you gain real-time insights into your spending patterns, enabling you to make informed decisions and stay accountable to your budget.

Comparison Shopping Techniques:

Smart spending involves making informed choices about where and how you spend your money. This section explores comparison shopping techniques, empowering you to find the best value for your purchases. Whether it's researching prices, seeking discounts, or considering alternatives, strategic comparison shopping enhances your spending efficiency.

Creating and Adhering to Spending Categories

Allocation for Discretionary Spending:

A strategic budget involves the allocation of funds to discretionary spending categories. We delve into the art of setting limits and guidelines for non-essential expenses. By defining spending categories, you create a structure that allows for enjoyment while maintaining financial discipline.

Regular Review and Adjustments:

Smart spending isn't a one-time endeavor; it's an ongoing process. This section emphasizes the importance of regular reviews and adjustments to your spending categories. By staying vigilant and adapting your allocations to changing circumstances, you ensure that your budget remains a dynamic and effective tool.

Leveraging Rewards Programs and Cash Back

Strategic Use of Credit Card Rewards:

Credit card rewards and cash-back programs can be strategic allies in your smart spending journey. We explore how to leverage these programs to your advantage, maximizing benefits without falling into the pitfalls of excessive debt. When used wisely, rewards become a valuable addition to your financial toolkit.

Mindful Approach to Loyalty Programs:

While loyalty programs can offer perks, a mindful approach is essential. This section discusses the strategic use of loyalty programs without succumbing to unnecessary spending. By navigating loyalty programs with intention, you extract value without compromising your budgetary goals.

Implementing No-Spend Challenges

Periodic No-Spend Challenges:

A powerful strategy for recalibrating spending habits is the implementation of no-spend challenges. This section explores the concept of temporarily abstaining from non-essential expenses. By undertaking periodic no-spend challenges, you gain a fresh perspective on your relationship with money and break patterns of unnecessary spending.

Reflecting on Value and Impact:

During no-spend challenges, reflection becomes a key component. We discuss the importance of evaluating the value and impact of your spending choices. By questioning the necessity of each expense, you develop a heightened awareness that extends beyond the challenge period, influencing your long-term spending behavior.

Fostering Financial Literacy and Education

Continuous Learning about Personal Finance:

Smart spending is fueled by financial literacy. We delve into the significance of continuous learning about personal finance. Whether it's staying informed about investment opportunities, understanding market trends, or enhancing your knowledge of budgeting strategies, ongoing education empowers you to make smarter spending decisions.

Seeking Professional Guidance:

For complex financial decisions, seeking professional guidance can be invaluable. This section discusses the role of financial advisors in providing insights and strategies tailored to your specific situation. By tapping into expert advice, you enhance your ability to make informed and intelligent spending choices.

As you embark on the exploration of strategies for smart spending, envision yourself not just as a consumer but as a curator of a life rich in financial well-being. By the end of this section, you will have acquired a palette of smart spending strategies, transforming your budget into a canvas where every financial choice contributes to the masterpiece of your overall financial success.

- Balancing Enjoyment and Financial Responsibility

In the symphony of financial mastery, striking the delicate balance between enjoyment and financial responsibility becomes the crescendo that defines your journey toward a life of abundance. This section delves into the artful process of navigating between fulfilling experiences and fiscal prudence, ensuring that every financial decision contributes to both joy and long-term financial well-being.

Defining Financial Priorities

Clarifying Personal Values:

Balancing enjoyment and financial responsibility begins with a deep dive into your values. We explore how aligning your spending choices with your values provides a foundation for intentional decision-making. By defining what truly matters to you, you set the stage for a budget that reflects your aspirations and priorities.

Setting Clear Financial Goals:

Goals are the compass that guides your financial journey. This section emphasizes the importance of setting clear and achievable financial goals. Whether it's saving for a dream vacation, building an emergency fund, or investing for the future, goals provide direction and purpose to your budgeting efforts.

Allocating Resources Mindfully

Categorizing Needs and Wants:

A key element in balancing enjoyment and financial responsibility lies in categorizing your expenses into needs and wants. We delve into the art of distinguishing between essential expenditures and discretionary spending. By allocating resources mindfully, you ensure that both immediate needs and personal pleasures are addressed in your budget.

Establishing Spending Limits:

Limits become the guardrails that guide your financial journey. This section explores the strategic establishment of spending limits for discretionary categories. By setting clear boundaries, you create a framework that allows for enjoyment while preventing overspending that may compromise your financial goals.

Incorporating Joyful Spending

Budgeting for Enjoyment:

Financial responsibility doesn't equate to deprivation. We discuss the importance of budgeting for enjoyment, and allocating resources intentionally to experiences that bring joy and fulfilment. Whether it's a hobby, travel, or entertainment, joyful spending becomes an integral part of your budgeting strategy.

Identifying High-Impact Enjoyment:

Not all enjoyable experiences carry the same weight. This section explores the concept of high-impact enjoyment—identifying activities that bring maximum satisfaction relative to their cost. By focusing on experiences with lasting value, you amplify the impact of your joyful spending within the constraints of your budget.

Strategies for Responsible Enjoyment

Mindful Spending Decisions:

The heart of balancing enjoyment and financial responsibility lies in making mindful spending decisions. We explore strategies for evaluating the necessity and impact of each expense. By adopting a thoughtful approach to spending, you ensure that your financial choices contribute to your overall well-being.

Prioritizing Debt Reduction:

Responsible financial behavior includes addressing existing debts. This section discusses the importance of prioritizing debt reduction within your budget. By allocating resources to paying down debts, you create a foundation for long-term financial stability and open avenues for increased enjoyment in the future.

Adaptability in Financial Planning

Flexibility in the Face of Life Changes:

Life is dynamic, and so is your financial journey. We delve into the concept of flexibility in financial planning. Whether it's adapting to changes in income, expenses, or personal circumstances, a flexible approach ensures that your budget remains resilient in the face of life's fluctuations.

Periodic Reviews and Adjustments:

Balancing enjoyment and financial responsibility requires periodic reviews of your budget. This section emphasizes the importance of regular assessments and adjustments. By staying attuned to changes in your financial landscape, you empower yourself to refine your budget, ensuring it remains aligned with your evolving priorities.

Celebrating Financial Milestones

Acknowledging Achievements:

Every step toward balancing enjoyment and financial responsibility is an achievement. This section encourages you to acknowledge and celebrate your milestones. Whether it's reaching a savings goal, reducing debt, or successfully adhering to spending limits, recognizing your accomplishments reinforces positive financial habits.

Transitioning to New Financial Chapters:

As you successfully balance enjoyment and financial responsibility, you transition to new financial chapters. This could involve setting loftier goals, exploring new experiences, or redirecting resources toward different priorities. Balancing becomes a dynamic and evolving process, ensuring that your financial journey remains fulfilling and purposeful.

As you navigate the art of balancing enjoyment and financial responsibility, envision yourself not just as a budgeter but as a conductor orchestrating a harmonious symphony of financial well-being. By the end of this section, you will have mastered the art of making financial choices that not only bring joy to your present but also contribute to the sustainable and prosperous future you envision.

- Strategic Saving Techniques

In the pursuit of financial mastery, saving transcends a mere financial task to become the brushstroke that paints a canvas of resilience and opportunity. This section unveils strategic saving techniques, guiding you to transform your financial aspirations into a tangible reality by cultivating a robust foundation of savings.

 Embracing the Pay Yourself First Principle

Priority for Savings Contributions:

The essence of strategic saving lies in embracing the "Pay Yourself First" principle. We delve into the importance of prioritizing savings contributions at the forefront of your budget. By allocating a portion of your income to savings before addressing other expenses, you establish a foundation for financial growth.

Automating Savings Contributions:

Consistency is the key to successful strategic saving. This section explores the power of automation, encouraging you to set up automatic transfers to your savings accounts. By automating contributions, you transform saving into a nonnegotiable habit, ensuring a steady and disciplined approach to building your financial foundation.

Creating a Multi-Tiered Savings Structure

Emergency Fund as the Foundation:

A strategic savings structure begins with the establishment of an emergency fund. We discuss the pivotal role of an emergency fund in providing financial security and stability. By prioritizing the creation of this foundation, you shield yourself from unforeseen challenges and create a platform for further financial growth.

Short-Term Goals for Immediate Wins:

Strategic saving involves breaking down larger objectives into achievable short-term goals. This section guides you in creating short-term savings targets that offer immediate wins. Whether it's a vacation, a home appliance, or a personal treat, accomplishing short-term goals reinforces positive saving habits.

Long-Term Investments for Future Wealth:

Looking to the future, strategic saving extends to long-term investments. We explore the importance of earmarking funds for investments that align with your financial goals. Whether it's retirement, education, or wealth-building, long-term investments become the pillars supporting your financial journey.

Maximizing Savings with Frugality

Mindful Spending and Cost-Cutting:

Strategic saving incorporates elements of frugality. We discuss the significance of mindful spending and cost-cutting strategies. By evaluating your spending habits and identifying areas where expenses can be reduced, you maximize the impact of your savings contributions, accelerating your progress toward financial goals.

Budget Surpluses as Savings Opportunities:

Surpluses in your budget provide strategic opportunities for savings. This section explores how to leverage budget surpluses by channeling them into your savings accounts. Whether it's from reduced expenses or unexpected windfalls, capitalizing on surpluses enhances your ability to meet savings targets.

Leveraging High-Interest Savings Vehicles

Exploring High-Interest Savings Accounts:

Strategic saving involves optimizing the growth of your funds. We delve into the benefits of high-interest savings accounts. By exploring accounts that offer competitive interest rates, you amplify the returns on your savings, accelerating the accumulation of wealth over time.

Utilizing Tax-Advantaged Accounts:

Tax-advantaged accounts are strategic vehicles for long-term savings. This section discusses the advantages of utilizing accounts such as IRAs, 401(k)s, or other tax-advantaged options. By taking advantage of tax benefits, you enhance the efficiency of your savings strategy and position yourself for greater financial security.

Capitalizing on Windfalls and Bonuses

Allocating Windfalls to Savings:

Windfalls, whether from bonuses, tax refunds, or unexpected income, present strategic opportunities for savings. We explore the art of allocating windfalls directly to your savings accounts. By capitalizing on these financial boosts, you expedite your progress toward achieving savings goals.

Strategic Use of Bonuses:

Workplace bonuses can be strategic tools for boosting your savings. This section discusses how to strategically use bonuses, whether for accelerating debt repayment, bolstering your emergency fund, or contributing to long-term investments. By making intentional choices with bonuses, you maximize their impact on your financial goals.

Reviewing and Adjusting Savings Strategies

Regular Reviews of Savings Goals:

Strategic saving is an evolving process. We emphasize the importance of regular reviews of your savings goals. By assessing your progress and adjusting targets as needed, you ensure that your savings strategy remains aligned with your changing financial landscape.

Adapting to Life Changes:

Life is dynamic, and strategic saving requires adaptability. This section explores how to navigate life changes such as job transitions, income fluctuations, or new financial priorities. By adapting your savings strategy to evolving circumstances, you fortify the resilience of your financial plan.

Celebrating Savings Milestones

Acknowledging Savings Achievements:

Every milestone in your savings journey is a cause for celebration. This section encourages you to acknowledge and celebrate your savings achievements. Whether it's reaching a specific savings target or consistently adhering to your savings plan, recognizing your progress reinforces positive financial habits.

Transitioning to New Saving Horizons:

As you reach and surpass savings milestones, you transition to new horizons in your financial journey. This could involve setting loftier goals, exploring new investment opportunities, or redirecting savings toward different priorities. Strategic saving becomes a dynamic and ongoing process, ensuring that your financial journey evolves with you.

As you immerse yourself in the process of strategic saving techniques, envision yourself not just as a saver but as a sculptor shaping a financial masterpiece. By the end of this section, you will have honed the skills of intentional saving, crafted a resilient financial foundation, and positioned yourself to realize the wealth of opportunities that strategic saving affords.

- Automating Savings

In the orchestration of financial mastery, automating savings emerges as a powerful melody that ensures consistency, discipline, and the steady crescendo of your financial well-being. This section delves into the strategic process of automating your savings, transforming a routine task into a symphony of financial success.

Understanding the Power of Automation

Consistency through Automation:

The foundation of strategic saving lies in the power of consistency. We explore how automating savings enables you to establish a reliable and disciplined approach to building your financial foundation. By removing the need for manual transfers, automation ensures that your savings contributions occur seamlessly and predictably.

Overcoming Procrastination:

Procrastination can be a formidable obstacle to saving. This section discusses how automation serves as a potent antidote to procrastination. By setting up automatic transfers, you eliminate the need for active decision-making, making saving a passive and integral part of your financial routine.

Setting Up Automated Transfers

Linking Accounts for Seamless Transfers:

The process of automating savings begins with linking your accounts. We guide you through the steps of setting up automated transfers between your checking and savings accounts. By establishing this connection, you create a streamlined path for the consistent flow of funds into your savings.

Defining Transfer Frequencies:

Automated transfers come with flexibility in defining transfer frequencies. This section explores the options for setting up transfers—whether it's a monthly, bi-weekly, or weekly schedule. By aligning transfer frequencies with your income schedule, you tailor the automation to suit your financial cadence.

Allocating Funds to Specific Goals

Goal-Oriented Automation:

Strategic saving involves allocating funds to specific goals. We discuss how to incorporate goal-oriented automation by designating transfers for different objectives. Whether it's an emergency fund, a vacation fund, or long-term investments, goal-oriented automation ensures that your savings align with your financial aspirations.

Creating Multiple Savings Buckets:

To enhance specificity, consider creating multiple savings buckets. This section explores the concept of designating separate accounts or sub-accounts for different goals. By visualizing your savings as distinct buckets, you gain clarity on progress toward each objective and can easily track and manage your financial goals.

Leveraging Employer Payroll Systems

Direct Deposit for Employer-Based Savings:

For those with employer-based income, leveraging direct deposit becomes a strategic tool for automated savings. We discuss the advantages of directing a portion of your paycheck directly into your savings account. By integrating savings into your payroll system, you ensure that your financial goals are prioritized from the moment you receive your income.

Exploring Employer Retirement Plans:

Employer-sponsored retirement plans, such as 401(k)s, offer additional avenues for automated savings. This section explores how contributions to retirement accounts can be automated directly from your paycheck. By participating in employer-sponsored plans, you capitalize on tax advantages and foster a disciplined approach to long-term savings.

Monitoring and Adjusting Automation

Regular Reviews of Automated Transfers:

Automated savings don't mean a "set it and forget it" mentality. Regular reviews are essential. We discuss the importance of periodically assessing your automated transfers. By ensuring that the amounts align with your current financial situation and goals, you maintain control and adaptability in your savings strategy.

Adjusting for Life Changes:

Life is dynamic, and your financial landscape may change. This section explores the necessity of adjusting automated transfers in response to life changes such as income fluctuations, new financial priorities, or changes in goals. By adapting your automated savings to evolving circumstances, you optimize the effectiveness of your strategy.

Celebrating Automated Savings Success

Acknowledging Milestones:

Every step in your automated savings journey is a milestone. This section encourages you to acknowledge and celebrate your savings achievements. Whether it's reaching a specific savings target or consistently adhering to your automated plan, recognizing your progress reinforces positive financial habits.

As you experience success with automated savings, you transition to new savings chapters. This could involve setting higher goals, exploring new investment opportunities, or redirecting savings toward different priorities. Automated savings become a dynamic and evolving process, ensuring that your financial journey continues to thrive.

By embracing the process of automating savings, envision yourself not just as a saver but as a conductor orchestrating a symphony of financial success. By the end of this section, you will have mastered the art of automated savings, creating a harmonious rhythm that propels you toward your financial goals with consistency, discipline, and the assurance of a well-designed financial future.

- Maximizing Savings through Smart Banking

In the intricate composition of financial mastery, the process of maximizing savings through smart banking takes center stage. This section unravels the strategic interplay between your banking choices and savings objectives, guiding you to leverage smart banking practices to amplify the growth and efficiency of your financial foundation.

Choosing High-Interest Savings Accounts

Exploring High-Yield Options:

The process of maximizing savings begins with the careful selection of a high-interest savings account. We delve into the importance of exploring high-yield options offered by various financial institutions. By securing a savings account with a competitive interest rate, you maximize the returns on your savings, accelerating your wealth accumulation.

Online Banks and Digital Platforms:

Consideration for online banks and digital platforms is integral to smart banking. This section explores the benefits of these institutions, such as lower fees and higher interest rates. By embracing the convenience and advantages of online banking, you position yourself for enhanced savings growth.

Capitalizing on Specialized Savings Accounts

Employer-Provided Savings Plans:

For those with employer-sponsored retirement plans, such as 401(k)s, maximizing savings involves active participation. We discuss the strategic advantage of contributing to employer-provided savings plans, capitalizing on potential employer matches and tax benefits to amplify your long-term savings.

Health Savings Accounts (HSAs):

The intersection of health and wealth brings forth the importance of Health Savings Accounts (HSAs). This section explores how contributing to an HSA can serve as a dual-purpose strategy—addressing healthcare costs while maximizing tax-advantaged savings. By leveraging HSAs, you integrate health considerations into your smart banking approach.

Implementing Automated Savings Transfers

Direct Deposit Allocation:

A seamless integration of smart banking with strategic saving lies in the allocation of direct deposits. We discuss the benefits of automating savings transfers directly from your paycheck. By earmarking a portion of your income for savings before it reaches your spending account, you embed a consistent and disciplined approach to building your financial foundation.

Automated Transfers between Accounts:

Beyond direct deposit, the process of maximizing savings involves setting up automated transfers between accounts. This section guides you through the steps of automating transfers between checking and savings accounts. By incorporating automation, you ensure a systematic and predictable flow of funds into your savings, fostering financial consistency.

Leveraging Cashback and Rewards Programs

Strategic Credit Card Usage:

Smart banking extends to strategic credit card usage. We explore how leveraging cashback and rewards programs can contribute to your savings. By making intentional choices in your credit card usage and maximizing rewards, you infuse an additional layer of savings into your financial strategy.

Aligning Rewards with Savings Goals:

The synergy between rewards and savings goals is a key consideration. This section discusses the strategic alignment of credit card rewards with specific savings objectives. Whether it's directing cashback toward an emergency fund or using travel rewards for a vacation fund, aligning rewards with goals enhances the impact on your overall savings.

Monitoring and Analyzing Banking Fees

Fee-Free Banking:

Smart banking involves a keen awareness of fees associated with your accounts. We delve into the importance of choosing fee-free banking options. By minimizing or eliminating account fees, you preserve more of your money, contributing to your overall savings goals.

Regular Review of Account Statements:

Ongoing monitoring is essential in the process of maximizing savings through smart banking. This section emphasizes the significance of regularly reviewing account statements. By scrutinizing transactions, fees, and interest rates, you maintain control over your financial landscape and identify opportunities for optimization.

Exploring Innovative Banking Technologies

Utilizing Budgeting Apps and Tools:

Innovation in banking technologies offers additional avenues for maximizing savings. We discuss the benefits of utilizing budgeting apps and tools provided by modern banking institutions. By leveraging these resources, you gain real-time insights into your spending patterns, identify areas for improvement, and enhance your overall financial management.

Digital Wallets and Round-Up Features:

The integration of digital wallets and round-up features represents the cutting edge of smart banking. This section explores how these technologies can contribute to your savings strategy. Whether it's rounding up purchases to the nearest dollar or utilizing cashback features, digital innovations offer inventive ways to augment your savings.

Celebrating Banking Milestones

Acknowledging Fee Savings and Rewards Accumulation:

Every achievement in your smart banking journey is a milestone. This section encourages you to acknowledge and celebrate fee savings, rewards accumulation, and other banking-related successes. By recognizing these milestones, you reinforce positive financial habits and maintain motivation on your journey to maximize savings.

Transitioning to New Banking Horizons:

As you experience success in maximizing savings through smart banking, you transition to new banking horizons. This could involve exploring advanced investment options, optimizing the use of rewards programs, or adapting to emerging banking technologies. Smart banking becomes a dynamic and evolving process, ensuring that your financial journey continues to thrive.

By embracing the process of maximizing savings through smart banking, envision yourself not just as an account holder but as an architect designing a robust financial structure. By the end of this section, you will have harnessed the power of smart banking practices to fortify your savings, amplify your financial growth, and position yourself on the path to enduring financial success.

- Leveraging Technology for Financial Efficiency

In the symphony of financial mastery, the integration of technology emerges as a powerful crescendo that transforms the complexities of budgeting and saving into a harmonious and efficient orchestration. This section delves into the strategic process of leveraging technology to enhance financial efficiency, providing you with a suite of tools and approaches to streamline your financial journey.

Embracing Budgeting Apps and Platforms

Real-Time Financial Insights:

The process of leveraging technology for financial efficiency begins with embracing budgeting apps and platforms. We explore how these tools provide real-time insights into your financial landscape, allowing you to track income, expenses, and savings with precision. By having a comprehensive view of your financial health, you gain the foundation for strategic decision-making.

Categorization and Analysis:

Budgeting apps facilitate the categorization and analysis of your spending patterns. This section guides you through the process of using these features to understand where your money is going. By leveraging technology for categorization and analysis, you identify opportunities for optimization and alignment with your financial goals.

Automating Savings and Investments

Automatic Transfers and Contributions:

Efficiency in savings is heightened through the automation of transfers and contributions. We discuss the strategic setup of automatic transfers between accounts and contributions to savings and investment accounts. By automating these processes, you not only ensure consistency but also free up time for strategic financial planning.

Robo-Advisors for Investment Efficiency:

The integration of robo-advisors represents a technological leap in investment efficiency. This section explores how these automated investment platforms use algorithms to optimize your investment portfolio. By leveraging robo-advisors, you benefit from efficient, low-cost investment management tailored to your risk tolerance and financial goals.

Utilizing Digital Wallets and Contactless Payments

Efficiency in Transactions:

Digital wallets and contactless payments usher in a new era of transactional efficiency. We discuss how these technologies streamline the payment process, providing convenience and speed. By adopting digital wallets, you simplify your transactions, reducing the friction associated with traditional payment methods.

Round-Up Features for Automatic Savings:

The integration of round-up features within digital wallets serves a dual purpose. This section explores how rounding up purchases to the nearest dollar and directing the spare change to savings can automate and optimize your savings strategy. By incorporating round-up features, you turn everyday transactions into opportunities for efficient savings.

Exploring High-Interest Online Banking

Online Banks for Higher Yields:

Efficiency in banking extends to exploring high-interest online banking options. We delve into the benefits of online banks, including higher yields and lower fees. By leveraging the efficiency of online banking, you maximize the returns on your savings and optimize your financial management.

Digital Platforms for Financial Aggregation:

Digital platforms that offer financial aggregation provide a centralized view of your accounts. This section discusses the advantages of using these platforms to consolidate information from various accounts, loans, and investments. By leveraging technology for financial aggregation, you streamline the monitoring and management of your financial portfolio.

Enhancing Security with Biometrics and Two-Factor Authentication

Biometric Authentication for Security:

Efficiency in financial management is intertwined with security. We explore the role of biometric authentication, such as fingerprint or facial recognition, in securing your financial accounts. By incorporating these advanced security measures, you ensure the protection of your financial information with a seamless and efficient user experience.

Two-Factor Authentication for Added Security Layers:

The integration of two-factor authentication adds an extra layer of security to your financial accounts.

This section discusses the importance of using two-factor authentication methods, such as codes sent to your mobile device, to safeguard your accounts. By embracing this technology, you fortify the security of your financial transactions.

Implementing Smart Contract Technologies

Efficient and Automated Contract Execution:

Smart contract technologies, based on blockchain, bring efficiency to financial agreements. We explore how these contracts, executed automatically when predefined conditions are met, streamline processes such as loan disbursements or investment transactions. By leveraging smart contract technologies, you reduce the need for intermediaries and enhance transactional efficiency.

Transparency and Security in Financial Agreements:

Beyond efficiency, smart contracts contribute to transparency and security in financial agreements.

This section discusses how the decentralized nature of blockchain ensures transparency, and the cryptographic security measures safeguard the integrity of financial contracts. By adopting smart contract technologies, you introduce trust and efficiency into your financial agreements.

Regularly Updating Financial Software

Software Updates for Enhanced Functionality:

Efficiency in leveraging technology requires the regular updating of financial software. We emphasize the importance of staying current with software updates to access enhanced functionality, improved security features, and compatibility with evolving financial technologies. By keeping your financial software up-to-date, you ensure optimal performance and efficiency.

Adaptability to Changing Financial Landscapes:

Financial landscapes evolve, and so should your technological tools. This section explores the adaptability of financial software to changing trends, regulations, and user needs. By choosing software that can seamlessly adapt to the dynamic nature of the financial industry, you future-proof your technological tools.

 Celebrating Technological Milestones

Acknowledging Efficiency Gains:

Every efficiency gain through technology is a milestone. This section encourages you to acknowledge and celebrate technological milestones, whether it's optimizing your budget with an app, automating savings transfers, or embracing innovative payment methods. By recognizing these achievements, you reinforce a tech-savvy approach to financial mastery.

Transitioning to New Technological Horizons:

As you experience success in leveraging technology for financial efficiency, you transition to new technological horizons. This could involve exploring emerging fintech solutions, adopting advanced investment platforms, or embracing cutting-edge financial technologies. Technological efficiency becomes a dynamic and evolving process, ensuring that your financial journey continues to advance.

By embracing the process of leveraging technology for financial efficiency, envision yourself not just as a user but as a navigator steering through the digital landscape of financial possibilities. By the end of this section, you will have harnessed the power of technology to streamline your financial processes, optimize your savings strategy, and position yourself as a conductor orchestrating an efficient and resilient financial symphony.

CHAPTER 4: NAVIGATING THE WORLD OF INVESTMENTS

In the expansive realm of financial mastery, the journey into the world of investments marks a pivotal chapter—one where strategic decisions can transform aspirations into tangible wealth. Welcome to a voyage that transcends the boundaries of saving, inviting you to explore the dynamic landscape of investments. In this chapter, we navigate through the intricacies, opportunities, and strategies that define the world of investments, empowering you to make informed choices and shape a prosperous financial future.

As we set sail into the world of investments, envision this chapter as your compass, guiding you through the diverse terrain of asset classes, risk management, and wealth-building strategies. Whether you're a seasoned investor seeking to refine your approach or a novice eager to embark on this financial odyssey, our exploration will illuminate the principles that underpin successful investing and equip you with the tools to navigate the complexities of the investment landscape.

Join us as we unravel the art of asset allocation, decipher the language of financial markets, and delve into the nuances of risk and return. From traditional investments like stocks and bonds to the avant-garde realms of cryptocurrencies and alternative assets, this chapter is designed to be your companion, offering insights, strategies, and a compass to navigate the twists and turns of the investment journey.

So, fasten your seatbelt, open your mind to the possibilities, and let's embark on a journey that transcends numbers and charts, where your financial aspirations meet the boundless potential of the investment world. As we navigate through this chapter, may you discover not only the art but also the science of investments, transforming your financial goals into a reality that reflects the mastery of wealth-building strategies. Welcome to the world of investments—where your financial future awaits exploration and discovery.

- Investment Basics

In the vast expanse of the financial universe, understanding the fundamentals of investments is akin to having a reliable compass that guides you through the complexities of wealth-building. This section serves as your foundational map, illuminating the core principles and essential concepts that constitute the bedrock of sound investment practices. Whether you're a novice investor taking your first steps or a seasoned player revisiting the basics, our exploration begins with a comprehensive overview of the fundamental building blocks of successful investing.

Defining Investments and Their Purpose

Investments as Wealth-Building Tools:

At its essence, an investment is more than a financial transaction; it's a strategic commitment to building wealth over time. We delve into the purpose of investments, exploring how they serve as powerful tools to grow capital, generate income, and achieve financial goals. Understanding the transformative potential of investments sets the stage for informed decision-making.

Balancing Risk and Reward:

One of the fundamental tenets of investments is the interplay between risk and reward. This section explores how risk and reward are inherently linked—higher potential returns often come with increased risk. By gaining insight into this delicate balance, you empower yourself to make investment choices aligned with your risk tolerance and financial objectives.

Types of Investments

Equities (Stocks):

Equities, commonly known as stocks, represent ownership in a company. We discuss the characteristics of stocks, their potential for capital appreciation, and the role they play in diversified investment portfolios. Understanding the dynamics of the stock market is essential for investors aiming for long-term growth.

Fixed-Income Securities (Bonds):

Bonds, or fixed-income securities, provide a contrasting element to stocks. This section explores how bonds function as debt instruments, offering regular interest payments and return of principal. Understanding the role of bonds in a portfolio contributes to effective risk management and income generation.

Real Assets and Real Estate:

Investment extends beyond traditional financial instruments. We delve into real assets, including real estate, as tangible investments with the potential for appreciation and income. Exploring the diversification benefits of real assets adds a layer of depth to your investment strategy.

Cash Equivalents:

Cash equivalents, such as money market funds, serve as a haven for liquidity and stability. This section examines how these instruments provide a safe parking place for funds while maintaining accessibility. Understanding the role of cash equivalents is crucial for effective cash management within an investment portfolio.

Investment Vehicles and Accounts

Mutual Funds and Exchange-Traded Funds (ETFs):

Investment vehicles like mutual funds and ETFs offer a convenient way to gain exposure to diversified portfolios. We explore the structures, benefits, and considerations associated with these popular investment options. Understanding these vehicles enhances your ability to tailor your investments to specific goals.

Individual Retirement Accounts (IRAs) and 401(k)s:

Retirement accounts, such as IRAs and 401(k)s, play a crucial role in long-term financial planning. This section delves into the features and advantages of these tax-advantaged accounts, emphasizing their significance in building a retirement nest egg.

The Importance of Diversification

Spreading Risk through Diversification:

Diversification emerges as a cornerstone of sound investment strategy. We discuss how spreading investments across different asset classes mitigates risk and enhances the potential for returns. Understanding the principles of diversification empowers you to construct resilient and balanced portfolios.

Investment Strategies and Approaches

Long-Term Investing:

A time-tested approach to investing is the long-term perspective. We explore the benefits of adopting a patient and strategic outlook, allowing investments to compound and weather short-term market fluctuations. Understanding the power of compounding is key to unlocking the full potential of long-term investing.

Value Investing and Growth Investing:

Investors often align with different philosophies, such as value investing or growth investing. This section dissects these approaches, highlighting how value investors seek undervalued assets, while growth investors focus on companies with high potential for expansion. Understanding these strategies enables you to align your investment style with your financial objectives.

Risk Management and Monitoring

Assessing and Managing Risk:

Risk is inherent in investing, but it can be managed. We discuss how to assess and manage risk by diversifying portfolios, setting realistic expectations, and staying informed. Understanding risk management strategies positions you to navigate the uncertainties of the market.

Regular Monitoring and Rebalancing:

Investment portfolios require periodic reviews and adjustments. This section emphasizes the importance of regular monitoring and rebalancing to ensure that your investments align with your goals and risk tolerance. Understanding the need for adaptability contributes to sustained portfolio health.

Investment Education and Resources

Continual Learning and Research:

Investing is an evolving landscape, and continual learning is paramount. We explore the importance of ongoing education and research to stay informed about market trends, economic indicators, and new investment opportunities. Understanding the value of knowledge positions you as an informed and proactive investor.

Utilizing Financial Advisors and Online Tools:

Financial advisors and online tools can be valuable resources for investors. This section discusses the benefits of seeking professional advice and leveraging online tools for research, analysis, and portfolio management. Understanding how to access and utilize these resources enhances your ability to make informed investment decisions.

Celebrating Investment Milestones

Acknowledging Portfolio Growth:

Every milestone in your investment journey is a cause for celebration. This section encourages you to acknowledge and celebrate moments of portfolio growth, achieving financial goals, and overcoming challenges. By recognizing these milestones, you reinforce positive investment habits and stay motivated on your path to financial success.

Transitioning to Advanced Investment Strategies:

As you gain experience and confidence, you may transition to advanced investment strategies. This could involve exploring options trading, alternative investments, or active trading. Understanding the possibilities of advanced strategies positions you to adapt your approach as your financial knowledge and goals evolve.

As we conclude this exploration of investment basics, envision yourself not just as an investor but as a navigator equipped with the knowledge to traverse the dynamic landscape of financial markets. By the end of this section, you will have gained a foundational understanding of investments, setting the stage for the more nuanced and advanced strategies that await in your journey through the world of investments.

- Stocks, Bonds, and Beyond

In the expansive universe of investments, a diversified portfolio is the compass that guides you through the terrain of financial opportunities. This section serves as your expedition into the intricacies of various asset classes, illuminating the distinctive characteristics, risk-return profiles, and strategic roles of stocks, bonds, and beyond. As we delve into this multifaceted landscape, envision a palette of investment instruments, each contributing its unique hue to the canvas of your wealth-building journey.

Understanding Stocks: Ownership in Companies

Equity Ownership and Shareholder Rights:

Stocks, or equities, represent ownership in companies. This section unravels the concept of equity ownership, detailing how owning stocks grants you a stake in a company. We explore the rights and privileges bestowed upon shareholders, emphasizing the role of stocks as instruments of long-term growth and participation in a company's success.

Common Stocks vs. Preferred Stocks:

Within the realm of stocks, distinctions exist between common and preferred stocks. We discuss the differences in ownership rights, dividends, and risk profiles associated with each type. Understanding these nuances empowers you to tailor your stock investments to align with your financial goals and risk tolerance.

Deciphering Bonds: Debt Instruments

Fixed-Income Characteristics:

Bonds, as fixed-income instruments, represent a different facet of the investment landscape. This section deciphers the characteristics of bonds, emphasizing their role as debt obligations issued by entities seeking capital. We explore how bonds provide regular interest payments and return of principal, making them integral components of income-focused portfolios.

Government Bonds, Corporate Bonds, and Municipal Bonds:

Diversity within the bond market extends to government bonds, corporate bonds, and municipal bonds. We delve into the distinctions among these bond types, considering factors such as issuer, risk, and tax implications. Understanding the nuances of each bond category enables you to construct a balanced and well-calibrated investment portfolio.

Venturing Beyond Traditional Assets

Real Assets: Real Estate and Commodities:

Beyond stocks and bonds, the investment landscape extends to real assets encompassing real estate and commodities. This section explores how investments in physical assets offer avenues for diversification and potential appreciation. Understanding the dynamics of real assets broadens your investment toolkit and enhances your portfolio resilience.

Cryptocurrencies and Alternative Investments:

Venturing into the contemporary realm of investments involves considering cryptocurrencies and alternative assets. We discuss the characteristics, risks, and evolving landscape of these unconventional instruments. Understanding the role of cryptocurrencies and alternative investments prepares you to navigate the dynamic and evolving nature of financial markets.

Evaluating Risk and Return

Risk-Return Profiles of Different Asset Classes:

Each asset class carries a distinct risk-return profile. This section evaluates the risk and return characteristics of stocks, bonds, real assets, and alternative investments. Understanding these profiles is essential for constructing a well-balanced portfolio that aligns with your financial goals and risk tolerance.

Correlation and Diversification:

The strategic interplay between asset classes involves correlation and diversification. We explore how combining assets with low or negative correlations can enhance portfolio diversification, mitigating risk. Understanding the principles of correlation and diversification empowers you to build resilient portfolios capable of weathering various market conditions.

Constructing a Diversified Portfolio

Asset Allocation Strategies:

The art of constructing a diversified portfolio revolves around asset allocation. This section delves into various asset allocation strategies, including strategic asset allocation, tactical asset allocation, and dynamic asset allocation. Understanding how to strategically distribute investments across asset classes optimizes your portfolio for long-term success.

Balancing Growth and Income Objectives:

Investors often balance growth and income objectives within their portfolios. This section explores how the allocation between growth-oriented and income-generating assets influences overall portfolio dynamics. Understanding the art of balancing growth and income positions you to create portfolios that align with your financial aspirations.

Tactical Approaches to Stock Investing

Value Investing and Growth Investing Strategies:

Within the realm of stock investing, tactical approaches like value investing and growth investing provide distinct strategies. We explore the principles of value investing, focusing on undervalued stocks, and growth investing, centered on companies with high growth potential. Understanding these approaches empowers you to tailor your stock investments to align with your investment philosophy.

Dividend Investing:

Dividend investing is a strategic approach that emphasizes the consistent income generated by stocks through dividends. This section discusses how selecting dividend-paying stocks can contribute to income streams and long-term wealth accumulation. Understanding the principles of dividend investing adds a layer of stability to your stock portfolio.

Embracing Global and Emerging Markets

Global Diversification:

Investors can broaden their horizons by embracing global diversification. This section explores the benefits and considerations associated with investing in international markets. Understanding the dynamics of global diversification enhances your ability to capture opportunities and manage risks on a global scale.

Exploring Emerging Markets:

Emerging markets offer unique opportunities for growth but come with distinct risks. We discuss the considerations involved in exploring investments in emerging economies. Understanding the dynamics of emerging markets empowers you to make informed decisions in pursuit of growth and diversification.

Navigating Market Cycles and Economic Trends

Cyclical and Defensive Assets:

Market cycles and economic trends influence the performance of different assets. This section explores cyclical and defensive assets and how their dynamics vary across economic phases. Understanding the characteristics of cyclical and defensive assets enables you to navigate market cycles with a proactive investment strategy.

Sector Rotation Strategies:

Investors often employ sector rotation strategies to capitalize on changing economic conditions. We delve into how sector rotation involves adjusting portfolio allocations based on the relative strength of different sectors. Understanding sector rotation strategies enhances your ability to align your investments with evolving economic trends.

The Importance of Research and Due Diligence

Conducting Fundamental Analysis:

In the realm of investments, research and due diligence are essential. This section emphasizes the importance of conducting fundamental analysis, including evaluating financial statements, understanding business models, and assessing competitive landscapes. Understanding the principles of fundamental analysis empowers you to make informed investment decisions.

Utilizing Technical Analysis:

Technical analysis complements fundamental analysis by examining price charts and market trends. This section explores the principles of technical analysis, including chart patterns and indicators. Understanding technical analysis provides a comprehensive toolkit for evaluating potential entry and exit points in the market.

Adapting to Market Volatility

Behavioral Finance and Emotional Intelligence:

Market volatility often triggers emotional responses among investors. This section explores the principles of behavioral finance and the importance of emotional intelligence in navigating turbulent markets. Understanding how emotions influence decision-making positions you to make rational and informed choices during periods of volatility.

Strategies for Volatile Markets:

Investors can employ specific strategies to navigate volatile markets. This section discusses approaches such as dollar-cost averaging, setting stop-loss orders, and rebalancing during market fluctuations.

Understanding these strategies equips you to adapt to changing market conditions with resilience and strategic poise.

Celebrating Investment Exploration

Acknowledging Portfolio Diversity:

Every exploration into diverse asset classes is a cause for celebration. This section encourages you to acknowledge and celebrate the diversity within your investment portfolio. By recognizing the unique contributions of each asset class, you reinforce a well-rounded and resilient approach to wealth-building.

Transitioning to Advanced Investment Strategies:

As your investment journey progresses, you may transition to advanced strategies, exploring options trading, derivatives, or alternative investments. Understanding the possibilities of advanced strategies positions you to adapt your approach as your financial knowledge and goals evolve.

As we conclude this journey through stocks, bonds, and beyond, envision yourself not just as an investor but as an architect of a well-crafted and diversified portfolio. By the end of this section, you will have gained a comprehensive understanding of various asset classes, paving the way for more advanced strategies and nuanced approaches in your quest for financial mastery.

- Risk Tolerance and Diversification

In the intricate dance of investments, two crucial partners—risk tolerance and diversification—take center stage, shaping the resilience and success of your financial journey. This section is a deep dive into the symbiotic relationship between your comfort with risk and the strategic art of diversification. As we navigate through these intertwined concepts, envision them as the twin engines propelling your portfolio toward stability, growth, and the achievement of your financial goals.

Understanding Risk Tolerance

Defining Risk Tolerance:

Risk tolerance is the bedrock upon which your investment strategy is built. This section illuminates the concept of risk tolerance—your ability and willingness to endure fluctuations in the value of your investments. We delve into the psychological and financial dimensions that influence your risk tolerance, setting the stage for constructing a portfolio aligned with your comfort level.

Assessing Personal Risk Tolerance:

The process of determining your risk tolerance involves introspection and assessment. We explore practical methods for evaluating your risk tolerance, considering factors such as financial goals, time horizon, and emotional temperament. Understanding your risk tolerance is a critical step in tailoring your investments to align with your unique financial profile.

The Risk-Return Relationship

Risk and Return Dynamics:

In the world of investments, risk and return are inseparable companions. This section explores the dynamic relationship between risk and potential reward, emphasizing the principle that higher potential returns often come with increased risk. Understanding this fundamental connection empowers you to make informed decisions that balance your risk appetite with your financial objectives.

Risk Categories in Investments:

Risk manifests in various forms within the realm of investments. We categorize risks, including market risk, credit risk, and liquidity risk, shedding light on the multifaceted nature of challenges that investors may encounter. Understanding the different risk categories equips you with the knowledge to navigate the complexities of the investment landscape.

Aligning Investments with Risk Tolerance

Matching Investments to Risk Preferences:

Investments exist on a spectrum of risk and return potential. This section guides you through the process of matching specific investments to your risk preferences. Whether you lean toward conservative, moderate, or aggressive strategies, aligning investments with your risk tolerance ensures a harmonious balance between stability and growth.

Building a Risk-Appropriate Portfolio:

Constructing a risk-appropriate portfolio involves strategic asset allocation. We explore how diversifying investments across different asset classes can moderate overall portfolio risk. Understanding the principles of asset allocation enables you to build a well-balanced portfolio that reflects your risk tolerance and financial goals.

The Art of Diversification

Defining Diversification:

Diversification is the investor's palette, blending various assets to create a resilient and balanced composition. This section illuminates the concept of diversification—spreading investments across different asset classes, industries, and geographic regions. We delve into how diversification acts as a risk management strategy, enhancing the potential for stable returns.

Benefits of Diversification:

The benefits of diversification extend beyond risk reduction. We explore how a diversified portfolio can enhance potential returns, mitigate the impact of poor-performing assets, and contribute to overall portfolio stability. Understanding the advantages of diversification positions you to harness its power for long-term financial success.

Strategies for Effective Diversification

Asset Class Diversification:

Diversifying across asset classes is a cornerstone of effective risk management. This section discusses the importance of including a mix of equities, fixed-income securities, and alternative assets in your portfolio. Understanding how different asset classes behave under various market conditions enhances the robustness of your diversification strategy.

Geographic and Sector Diversification:

Beyond asset classes, geographic and sector diversification further fortify your portfolio. We explore the strategic considerations of spreading investments across different regions and industries. Understanding the nuances of geographic and sector diversification adds layers of resilience to your investment approach.

Periodic Review and Rebalancing

Regular Portfolio Assessment:

The landscape of investments evolves, necessitating periodic portfolio assessments. This section emphasizes the importance of regularly reviewing your portfolio to ensure alignment with your risk tolerance and financial goals. Understanding the need for ongoing assessment positions you to adapt to changing market conditions.

Rebalancing Strategies:

Rebalancing is the fine-tuning of your portfolio to maintain desired asset allocations. We discuss strategies for rebalancing, including calendar-based and threshold-based approaches. Understanding how and when to rebalance ensures that your portfolio remains on course, navigating fluctuations while staying true to your risk tolerance.

Customizing Diversification for Individual Goals

Lifecycle Investing:

Individual financial goals evolve over a lifetime, requiring a dynamic approach to diversification.

This section explores the concept of lifecycle investing—adjusting your portfolio's risk profile based on your stage in life and financial objectives. Understanding the principles of lifecycle investing tailors your diversification strategy to align with your unique journey.

Customizing Risk Management for Short-Term and Long-Term Goals:

Not all financial goals have the same time horizon. We discuss how customizing risk management for short-term and long-term goals involves distinct diversification strategies. Understanding the nuances of aligning risk with specific objectives optimizes your portfolio for the timelines associated with each goal.

Navigating Market Turbulence with Diversification

Diversification as a Risk Mitigation Tool:

Market turbulence is inevitable, but its impact can be mitigated through diversification. This section explores how a well-diversified portfolio acts as a risk mitigation tool during challenging market conditions. Understanding the protective role of diversification empowers you to navigate market turbulence with resilience.

Staying Disciplined During Market Fluctuations:

Discipline is a key attribute in adhering to your diversification strategy during market fluctuations. We discuss the psychological aspects of staying disciplined and maintaining a long-term perspective. Understanding the importance of discipline ensures that your diversification strategy remains steadfast amid the ebb and flow of market sentiment.

Celebrating the Harmony of Risk and Diversification

Acknowledging Portfolio Resilience:

Every moment of portfolio resilience is a triumph. This section encourages you to acknowledge and celebrate the harmony achieved through the interplay of risk tolerance and diversification. By recognizing the strength of your diversified portfolio, you reinforce a disciplined and strategic approach to navigating the complexities of the investment landscape.

Transitioning to Advanced Risk Management Strategies:

As your financial journey progresses, you may explore advanced risk management strategies, such as options strategies, derivatives, or dynamic hedging. Understanding the possibilities of advanced risk management equips you to adapt your approach as your financial knowledge and goals evolve.

As we conclude this exploration of risk tolerance and diversification, envision yourself not just as an investor but as a conductor orchestrating a harmonious symphony of investments. By the end of this section, you will have gained a profound understanding of the delicate balance between risk and diversification, positioning yourself for a journey of financial mastery where stability and growth coexist in perfect harmony.

- Choosing Investments Aligned with Your Goals

In the vast landscape of investments, the art of selection becomes a compass guiding you towards the realization of your financial aspirations. This section is a strategic exploration into the process of choosing investments that harmonize with your unique goals. Envision this journey as a personalized roadmap, where each investment is a waypoint, propelling you closer to your envisioned destination of financial success.

Defining Your Financial Goals

Clarity in Goal Setting:

The first step in choosing investments aligned with your goals involves defining your financial aspirations with precision. This section explores the importance of setting clear, measurable, and time-bound goals. Understanding the significance of goal clarity establishes the foundation for selecting investments that resonate with your overarching financial vision.

Categorizing Short-Term and Long-Term Goals:

Financial goals span different time horizons, necessitating a categorization into short-term and long-term objectives. We delve into the process of distinguishing goals based on their temporal nature and explore how this categorization influences investment choices. Understanding the distinctions between short-term and long-term goals shapes the trajectory of your investment strategy.

Assessing Risk Tolerance

Mapping Risk Tolerance to Goals:

Risk tolerance is a dynamic factor that varies across individuals and goals. This section guides you through the process of mapping your risk tolerance to specific financial goals. We explore how different goals may warrant different risk levels, aligning your risk appetite with the nature of each aspiration. Understanding this mapping ensures that your investments reflect a customized balance of risk and return.

Considering Emotional and Financial Capacity:

Risk tolerance encompasses both emotional resilience and financial capacity. We discuss the importance of considering not only your psychological comfort with risk but also your financial ability to absorb fluctuations. Understanding the interplay between emotional and financial capacity refines your risk assessment and informs your investment decisions.

Matching Investments to Goal Time Horizons

Aligning Time Horizons with Asset Classes:

Different asset classes exhibit varying levels of volatility and return potential over time. This section explores the strategic alignment of asset classes with the time horizons of your goals. We delve into how equities, fixed-income securities, and alternative investments may be selected based on the anticipated duration until each goal is realized. Understanding this alignment optimizes the performance of your portfolio.

Dynamic Asset Allocation for Evolving Goals:

As your goals evolve, so should your asset allocation. We discuss the concept of dynamic asset allocation, emphasizing the need to periodically reassess and adjust your investment mix. Understanding the adaptability of asset allocation ensures that your portfolio remains in sync with the changing timelines and priorities of your goals.

Tailoring Investment Strategies to Specific Goals

Income-Generating Strategies for Short-Term Goals:

Short-term goals often demand a focus on capital preservation and regular income. This section explores income-generating investment strategies, including dividend-paying stocks and fixed-income securities, as suitable choices for short-term objectives. Understanding the income-generating potential of specific investments enhances the stability of your portfolio for immediate financial needs.

Growth-Oriented Strategies for Long-Term Goals:

Long-term goals provide the luxury of embracing growth-oriented strategies. We discuss how investments in equities and other high-growth assets can be tailored to maximize long-term wealth accumulation. Understanding the principles of growth-oriented strategies positions your portfolio for the potential appreciation needed to achieve expansive financial objectives.

Conducting Thorough Investment Research

Fundamental Analysis for In-Depth Evaluation:

Thorough research is the cornerstone of informed investment decisions. This section explores the principles of fundamental analysis—scrutinizing the financial health, management, and competitive positioning of potential investments. Understanding how to conduct in-depth fundamental analysis empowers you to make well-founded choices aligned with your goals.

Risk-Reward Assessment:

Each investment presents a unique risk-return profile. We discuss the process of assessing the risk-reward dynamics of potential investments, considering factors such as historical performance, volatility, and growth prospects. Understanding how to weigh risk against potential returns ensures that your investment choices align with your risk tolerance and financial objectives.

Diversification Strategies for Goal-Centric Portfolios

Diversification Tailored to Goals:

Diversification is not a one-size-fits-all concept; it should be tailored to your specific goals. This section explores how diversifying across asset classes, industries, and geographic regions can be strategically adjusted based on the nature of your goals. Understanding the customization of diversification ensures that your portfolio is resilient and optimized for each financial aspiration.

Goal-Centric Portfolio Construction:

The construction of a goal-centric portfolio involves weaving together investments in a manner that aligns with the desired outcomes. We discuss how to assemble a portfolio that reflects the risk tolerance, time horizon, and growth potential associated with each goal. Understanding the intricacies of goal-centric portfolio construction ensures that your investments work harmoniously towards achieving specific financial milestones.

Monitoring and Adjusting Your Investment Strategy

Regular Portfolio Monitoring:

Once investments are in motion, continuous monitoring becomes essential. This section emphasizes the importance of regularly reviewing your portfolio's performance relative to your goals. Understanding the need for ongoing monitoring positions you to identify opportunities, address challenges, and ensure that your investments remain on track.

Adjusting Strategies in Response to Goal Changes:

Goals are dynamic, and your investment strategy should be responsive to changes in your financial objectives. We discuss the process of adjusting your investment strategies in response to shifts in goals, timelines, or priorities. Understanding the adaptability of your investment approach ensures that your portfolio evolves in tandem with your changing financial landscape.

Seeking Professional Guidance for Complex Goals

Utilizing Financial Advisors for Specialized Goals:

Some financial goals may require specialized expertise. This section explores the benefits of seeking guidance from financial advisors for complex or intricate goals. Understanding when to leverage professional assistance enhances your ability to navigate intricate financial scenarios with confidence.

Aligning Investment Strategies with Tax Planning:

Tax planning is an integral part of goal-aligned investing. We discuss the importance of aligning your investment strategies with tax planning initiatives to optimize returns and minimize tax liabilities. Understanding the intersection between investment decisions and tax implications ensures a holistic and efficient approach to wealth management.

Celebrating Goal Achievements

Acknowledging Milestones:

Every goal achievement, no matter how small, is a triumph. This section encourages you to acknowledge and celebrate the milestones reached on your financial journey. By recognizing these achievements, you reinforce positive financial habits and cultivate a mindset of success.

Transitioning to New Financial Horizons:

As you achieve goals, new horizons emerge. We discuss the process of transitioning to new financial objectives, whether they involve expanding investments, diversifying further, or setting ambitious new goals. Understanding the transitions between financial horizons ensures that your journey is one of continual growth and accomplishment.

As we conclude this exploration of choosing investments aligned with your goals, envision yourself not just as an investor but as an architect crafting a portfolio tailored to your unique financial blueprint. By the end of this section, you will have gained a profound understanding of the meticulous process of aligning investments with your goals, paving the way for a journey where financial success and strategic choices harmonize in perfect unity.

- Building a Diversified Investment Portfolio

In the symphony of investment strategies, building a diversified portfolio emerges as a crescendo—a harmonious composition that orchestrates resilience, growth, and risk management. This section is an in-depth exploration of the meticulous process of constructing a diversified investment portfolio. Envision this journey as a curator selecting a palette of assets, each contributing a unique hue to the canvas of your financial success.

Understanding the Essence of Diversification

Defining Diversification:

Diversification is not just a strategy; it's a philosophy that forms the core of prudent investing. This section illuminates the essence of diversification—spreading investments across a variety of asset classes, industries, and geographic regions. We delve into how diversification acts as a risk management tool, mitigating the impact of poor-performing assets and enhancing the potential for stable returns.

Benefits of Diversification:

The benefits of diversification extend beyond risk reduction. We explore how a well-diversified portfolio can enhance potential returns, foster stability, and offer a smoother ride through market fluctuations. Understanding the advantages of diversification positions you to craft a portfolio that aligns with your financial goals and risk tolerance.

Crafting a Strategic Asset Allocation

Aligning Asset Allocation with Goals:

The foundation of a diversified portfolio is strategic asset allocation. This section guides you through the process of aligning asset allocation with your financial goals, risk tolerance, and time horizon. We explore how different asset classes, including equities, fixed-income securities, and alternative investments, contribute to a balanced and goal-centric portfolio.

Tailoring Asset Mix to Risk Tolerance:

Risk tolerance plays a pivotal role in shaping asset allocation. We discuss the strategic tailoring of the asset mix to align with your risk tolerance, ensuring that the portfolio reflects a customized balance of stability and growth. Understanding the symbiotic relationship between risk tolerance and asset allocation refines your approach to constructing a resilient portfolio.

Selecting Diverse Asset Classes

Equities:

Equities, or stocks, represent ownership in companies and offer potential for capital appreciation. This section explores the characteristics of equities, their role in a diversified portfolio, and strategic considerations for selecting individual stocks or equity funds. Understanding the dynamics of equities is fundamental to leveraging their growth potential.

Fixed-Income Securities:

Fixed-income securities, including bonds, provide stability and income. We delve into the world of fixed-income investments, discussing the role of bonds in diversification, their risk-return profile, and considerations for selecting bonds based on duration, credit quality, and yield. Understanding the nuances of fixed-income securities contributes to a well-balanced portfolio.

Real Assets:

Real assets, such as real estate and commodities, offer tangible diversification benefits. This section explores the strategic inclusion of real assets in a portfolio, considering their potential for appreciation and income. Understanding how real assets contribute to diversification broadens your investment toolkit.

Alternative Investments:

Venturing beyond traditional asset classes involves considering alternative investments. We discuss the characteristics, risks, and potential benefits of alternative investments such as hedge funds, private equity, and real assets. Understanding the role of alternative investments adds a layer of diversification to your portfolio.

Cash Equivalents:

Cash equivalents, such as money market funds, provide liquidity and stability. This section explores the role of cash equivalents in a diversified portfolio, serving as a haven and offering flexibility. Understanding how cash equivalents contribute to overall portfolio stability enhances your risk management strategy.

Geographic and Sector Diversification

Global Diversification:

Expanding the horizons of your portfolio involves global diversification. We discuss the benefits and considerations associated with investing in international markets, including exposure to diverse economies and currencies. Understanding the dynamics of global diversification enhances your ability to capture opportunities and manage risks on a global scale.

Sector Diversification:

Within equity investments, sector diversification further fortifies your portfolio. We explore the strategic considerations of spreading investments across different industries, considering factors such as economic cycles and sector-specific risks.

Understanding the nuances of sector diversification adds layers of resilience to your investment approach.

Fine-Tuning Diversification Strategies

Correlation and Diversification:

The effectiveness of diversification relies on understanding the correlation between asset classes. This section explores the principles of correlation and how combining assets with low or negative correlations enhances portfolio diversification. Understanding the strategic interplay between correlation and diversification refines your approach to building resilient portfolios.

Optimizing Diversification Through Rebalancing:

Diversification requires periodic attention to maintain optimal asset allocations. We discuss the importance of regular portfolio rebalancing—adjusting holdings to bring them back in line with the intended asset mix. Understanding the necessity of rebalancing ensures that your diversified portfolio remains aligned with your goals and risk tolerance.

Customizing Diversification for Personal Goals

Tailoring Diversification to Time Horizons:

Diversification should be tailored to the time horizons of your goals. This section explores how the dynamics of diversification may be adjusted based on whether goals are short-term or long-term. Understanding the customization of diversification ensures that your portfolio is optimized for the specific timelines associated with each financial aspiration.

Customizing Diversification for Risk Preferences:

Risk preferences vary among investors, influencing the depth and breadth of diversification. We discuss how diversification can be customized based on individual risk preferences, ensuring that the portfolio reflects a personalized balance of risk and return. Understanding the customization of diversification enhances the suitability of your portfolio for your unique financial profile.

Adapting Diversification to Market Conditions

Diversification as a Response to Market Conditions:

Market conditions evolve, requiring adaptability in diversification strategies. This section explores how diversification can be adjusted in response to changing economic trends, interest rates, and geopolitical events. Understanding the adaptability of diversification ensures that your portfolio remains resilient in the face of dynamic market conditions.

Sector Rotation Strategies:

Investors may employ sector rotation strategies to capitalize on changing economic conditions. We delve into how sector rotation involves adjusting portfolio allocations based on the relative strength of different sectors. Understanding sector rotation strategies enhances your ability to align your investments with evolving economic trends.

Incorporating Research and Due Diligence

Conducting Fundamental Analysis:

The foundation of informed investing lies in thorough research. This section emphasizes the importance of conducting a fundamental analysis—evaluating the financial health, competitive positioning, and growth prospects of potential investments. Understanding the principles of fundamental analysis empowers you to make well-founded choices within your diversified portfolio.

Utilizing Technical Analysis:

Technical analysis complements fundamental analysis by examining price charts and market trends. We explore the principles of technical analysis, including chart patterns and indicators. Understanding technical analysis provides a comprehensive toolkit for evaluating potential entry and exit points in the market.

Celebrating Portfolio Diversity

Acknowledging the Strength of Diversity:

Diversity within your portfolio is not just a feature; it's a strength to be celebrated. This section encourages you to acknowledge and appreciate the diversity within your investment holdings. By recognizing the unique contributions of each asset class, you reinforce a well-rounded and resilient approach to wealth-building.

Transitioning to Advanced Diversification Strategies:

As your investment journey progresses, you may explore advanced diversification strategies, including options trading, factor-based investing, or thematic investing. Understanding the possibilities of advanced strategies positions you to adapt your approach as your financial knowledge and goals evolve.

As we conclude this exploration of building a diversified investment portfolio, envision yourself not just as an investor but as a maestro orchestrating a symphony of diverse assets. By the end of this section, you will have gained a profound understanding of the meticulous process of constructing a well-balanced and resilient portfolio, setting the stage for a journey of financial mastery where stability and growth coexist in perfect harmony.

- Real Estate Investments

In the expansive realm of investments, real estate stands as a tangible cornerstone, offering a unique avenue for wealth creation, diversification, and long-term stability. This section delves into the intricacies of real estate investments, exploring the principles, strategies, and considerations that guide investors through the dynamic landscape of property ownership.

Understanding Real Estate as an Asset Class

Tangible Wealth:

Real estate, often hailed as "bricks and mortar," represents tangible wealth. This section explores how property ownership provides investors with a physical asset, fostering a sense of security and permanence. Understanding real estate as an asset class lays the foundation for harnessing its potential within a diversified investment portfolio.

Income Generation through Rental Properties:

One of the defining features of real estate is its capacity to generate income through rental properties. We delve into the strategic considerations of owning and leasing residential or commercial spaces, exploring how rental income contributes to a diversified and income-generating investment strategy.

Types of Real Estate Investments

Residential Real Estate:

Residential properties, including houses and apartments, form a significant segment of the real estate market. This section discusses the nuances of investing in residential real estate, from single-family homes to multifamily dwellings, emphasizing their role in providing stable rental income and potential for capital appreciation.

Commercial Real Estate:

Commercial properties, such as office buildings, retail spaces, and industrial facilities, offer distinct investment opportunities. We explore the considerations involved in commercial real estate investments, including leasing dynamics, location strategies, and the impact of economic trends on different commercial sectors.

Real Estate Investment Trusts (REITs):

Real Estate Investment Trusts (REITs) provide a unique vehicle for indirect real estate investment. This section discusses the structure of REITs, their benefits, and how they enable investors to access the real estate market without direct property ownership. Understanding the role of REITs adds a layer of flexibility to real estate investment strategies.

Key Considerations in Real Estate Investments

Location, Location, Location:

In real estate, the mantra is often "location, location, location." This section emphasizes the critical importance of location in property investment. We explore how factors such as neighborhood dynamics, proximity to amenities, and regional economic trends influence the desirability and potential appreciation of real estate assets.

Market Timing and Economic Trends:

Real estate markets are influenced by economic trends and cycles. We discuss the considerations involved in market timing, exploring how investors can strategically navigate economic shifts to optimize their real estate investments. Understanding the impact of broader economic trends on real estate markets enhances decision-making.

Financing and Leverage:

Financing plays a pivotal role in real estate investments, often involving the use of leverage. This section explores how investors can utilize mortgage financing to amplify their investment potential. Understanding the principles of financing and leverage equips investors to optimize capital deployment and enhance returns.

Strategies for Real Estate Investors

Buy-and-Hold Strategy:

The buy-and-hold strategy involves acquiring properties to hold them for an extended period. We discuss the benefits of this strategy, including long-term appreciation, steady rental income, and potential tax advantages. Understanding the dynamics of the buy-and-hold approach positions investors for sustained success in real estate.

Fix-and-Flip Strategy:

The fix-and-flip strategy involves purchasing properties, renovating or improving them, and selling them for a profit. This section explores the considerations involved in fix-and-flip investments, including property selection, renovation costs, and market timing. Understanding the intricacies of this strategy enables investors to navigate short-term real estate ventures.

Real Estate Crowdfunding:

The digital era has ushered in new avenues for real estate investment, including crowdfunding platforms. We discuss how real estate crowdfunding allows investors to pool resources for joint property ownership. Understanding the mechanics of crowdfunding expands the accessibility of real estate investments to a broader investor base.

Risks and Challenges in Real Estate Investments

Market Volatility and Liquidity:

Real estate investments, while stable over the long term, can be subject to market volatility and lack the liquidity of other asset classes. This section explores the risks associated with market fluctuations and the challenges investors may face in quickly liquidating real estate holdings. Understanding these aspects is crucial for balanced risk management.

Maintenance and Property Management:

Property ownership involves ongoing responsibilities, including maintenance and management. We discuss the challenges associated with property upkeep, tenant relations, and the importance of effective property management. Understanding these aspects prepares investors for the hands-on nature of real estate investments.

Interest Rate and Financing Risks:

Real estate investments are sensitive to interest rate fluctuations and financing risks. This section explores how changes in interest rates can impact property values and financing costs. Understanding the interplay between interest rates and real estate investments allows investors to navigate potential risks and opportunities.

Regulatory and Legal Considerations

Zoning and Regulatory Compliance:

Real estate investments are subject to zoning regulations and local ordinances. This section discusses the importance of understanding zoning laws and regulatory compliance when acquiring and developing properties. Awareness of these considerations is essential for avoiding legal complications.

Tax Implications of Real Estate Investments:

Real estate investments carry specific tax implications. We explore the tax advantages, such as depreciation and mortgage interest deductions, as well as the potential tax consequences of property sales. Understanding the tax landscape of real estate investments enables investors to optimize their financial outcomes.

Diversifying Real Estate Investments

Portfolio Diversification with Real Estate:

Real estate, as an asset class, offers diversification benefits. This section explores how incorporating real estate into an investment portfolio enhances overall diversification and risk mitigation. Understanding the role of real estate in portfolio construction contributes to a well-balanced and resilient investment strategy.

Global Real Estate Opportunities:

Investors can explore real estate opportunities beyond their local markets, tapping into global diversification. We discuss the considerations involved in international real estate investments, including currency dynamics and geopolitical factors. Understanding the possibilities of global real estate diversification broadens the scope of investment opportunities.

Sustainable and Responsible Real Estate Investing

Environmental, Social, and Governance (ESG) Factors:

Sustainable and responsible investing has gained prominence in the real estate sector. This section explores the integration of environmental, social, and governance (ESG) factors into real estate investment decisions. Understanding the impact of ESG considerations aligns real estate investments with broader sustainability goals.

Impact Investing in Real Estate:

Beyond financial returns, impact investing in real estate focuses on generating positive social and environmental outcomes. We discuss how investors can align their real estate portfolios with impactful initiatives, contributing to community development and environmental sustainability. Understanding the principles of impact investing adds a purpose-driven dimension to real estate strategies.

Celebrating Real Estate Success

Acknowledging Property Appreciation and Income Generation:

Every instance of property appreciation and income generation is a celebration of real estate success. This section encourages investors to acknowledge and appreciate the tangible outcomes of their real estate investments. By recognizing the dual benefits of property appreciation and income, investors reinforce a strategic and prosperous approach to real estate wealth-building.

Transitioning to Advanced Real Estate Strategies:

As investors gain experience, they may explore advanced real estate strategies, including commercial development, real estate syndications, or international property investments. Understanding the possibilities of advanced strategies positions investors to adapt their approach as their real estate knowledge and goals evolve.

As we conclude this exploration of real estate investments, envision yourself not just as an investor but as a steward of physical assets, navigating the diverse landscapes of residential, commercial, and global real estate. By the end of this section, you will have gained a profound understanding of the principles and strategies that underpin successful real estate investments, paving the way for a journey where tangible wealth and strategic choices harmonize in perfect unity.

- Entrepreneurship and Business Ventures

In the dynamic tapestry of investments, entrepreneurship and business ventures emerge as threads of innovation, risk-taking, and transformative wealth creation. This section delves into the intricacies of entrepreneurship, exploring the principles, challenges, and rewards of building and investing in businesses. Envision this journey as a landscape where entrepreneurs navigate the terrain of opportunity, creativity, and strategic vision.

Embracing Entrepreneurship as an Investment Avenue

The Entrepreneurial Mindset:

Entrepreneurship begins with a mindset—an appetite for risk, a passion for innovation, and a vision for creating value. This section explores the foundations of the entrepreneurial mindset, emphasizing the qualities that drive individuals to embark on the journey of building and investing in businesses. Understanding the essence of entrepreneurship sets the stage for a transformative investment experience.

Identifying Opportunities for Business Ventures:

Opportunities are the currency of entrepreneurship. We discuss how entrepreneurs and investors identify opportunities in the market, recognizing unmet needs, emerging trends, and gaps in existing solutions. Understanding the process of opportunity identification equips aspiring entrepreneurs and investors to spot potential avenues for business ventures.

The Entrepreneurial Journey

From Idea to Business Concept:

The journey from idea to business concept is a pivotal phase in entrepreneurship. This section explores how entrepreneurs refine their initial ideas into viable business concepts, considering market demand, competition, and feasibility. Understanding the iterative process of idea development lays the groundwork for turning concepts into thriving ventures.

Business Planning and Strategy:

A robust business plan is a compass guiding entrepreneurs through the complexities of business ownership. We delve into the elements of effective business planning, including market analysis, financial projections, and strategic positioning. Understanding the significance of business planning empowers entrepreneurs to articulate their vision and strategy to stakeholders.

Navigating Legal and Regulatory Landscapes:

Entrepreneurs must navigate legal and regulatory landscapes to ensure compliance and mitigate risks. This section explores the considerations involved in legal structures, intellectual property protection, and regulatory compliance. Understanding the legal dimensions of entrepreneurship safeguards business ventures and fosters long-term sustainability.

Funding and Capitalization

Bootstrapping and Self-Financing:

Bootstrapping, or self-financing, is a common starting point for entrepreneurs. We discuss how entrepreneurs use personal savings, revenue generated by the business, and minimal external financing to fund their ventures. Understanding the principles of bootstrapping instils financial discipline and resilience in the early stages of a business.

Seeking External Funding:

Entrepreneurs often seek external funding to scale their ventures. This section explores various sources of external funding, including angel investors, venture capitalists, and crowdfunding platforms. Understanding the dynamics of external funding empowers entrepreneurs to choose the most suitable financing options for their business goals.

Building Financial Models and Projections:

Financial models and projections are essential tools for attracting investors and making informed business decisions. We discuss the elements of financial modelling, including revenue forecasts, expense projections, and valuation considerations. Understanding how to build and interpret financial models enhances the credibility of entrepreneurs in the eyes of investors.

Scaling and Growth Strategies

Scalability and Sustainable Growth:

Scalability is the engine that propels businesses toward sustainable growth. This section explores how entrepreneurs design scalable business models and implement strategies for long-term growth.

Understanding the dynamics of scalability positions entrepreneurs to navigate the challenges of expansion while maintaining operational efficiency.

Strategic Partnerships and Alliances:

Strategic partnerships and alliances can accelerate business growth and open new avenues for collaboration. We discuss how entrepreneurs identify and cultivate partnerships that align with their strategic objectives. Understanding the value of strategic alliances enhances the agility and competitiveness of businesses in dynamic markets.

Innovation and Adaptation:

Innovation is the lifeblood of entrepreneurial ventures. This section explores how entrepreneurs foster a culture of innovation and adaptability, staying attuned to market trends and customer needs. Understanding the importance of continuous innovation equips businesses to thrive in evolving landscapes.

Challenges and Risk Management

Identifying and Mitigating Business Risks:

Every business venture involves inherent risks. We discuss how entrepreneurs identify and assess risks, developing strategies to mitigate potential challenges. Understanding the principles of risk management enables entrepreneurs to make informed decisions and safeguard the resilience of their ventures.

Market Competition and Differentiation:

Competing in crowded markets requires businesses to differentiate themselves effectively. This section explores how entrepreneurs navigate market competition, emphasizing the importance of unique value propositions and brand positioning. Understanding the dynamics of differentiation enhances the market relevance and visibility of businesses.

Adapting to Economic Shifts and Uncertainty:

Economic shifts and uncertainties are inevitable in the business landscape. We discuss how entrepreneurs adapt to changing economic conditions, implementing strategies for resilience and agility. Understanding how to navigate economic shifts positions businesses to weather challenges and seize opportunities in dynamic markets.

Exit Strategies and Succession Planning

Exit Strategies for Entrepreneurs:

Entrepreneurs often plan exit strategies to realize returns on their investments. This section explores various exit options, including selling the business, merging with other entities, or going public through an Initial Public Offering (IPO). Understanding exit strategies empowers entrepreneurs to make strategic decisions aligned with their long-term goals.

Succession Planning for Sustainable Businesses:

Building a legacy involves thoughtful succession planning. We discuss how entrepreneurs plan for the continuity of their businesses, whether through family succession, management buyouts, or other succession structures. Understanding the principles of succession planning ensures the sustainable growth and impact of businesses beyond the founder's tenure.

Entrepreneurship and Investment Portfolio

Incorporating Business Ventures into Investment Portfolios:

For investors, incorporating business ventures into their investment portfolios offers a unique avenue for diversification and potential high returns. This section explores how investors assess and integrate entrepreneurial opportunities into their broader investment strategies. Understanding the synergy between entrepreneurship and traditional investments enriches the diversity and growth potential of investment portfolios.

Balancing Risk and Reward in Business Investments:

Investing in businesses involves a balance of risk and reward. We discuss how investors evaluate the risk-return profiles of entrepreneurial ventures, considering factors such as industry dynamics, management capabilities, and growth potential. Understanding the principles of risk assessment enhances the strategic allocation of capital in business investments.

Impact Investing in Entrepreneurship:

Beyond financial returns, impact investing in entrepreneurship focuses on generating positive social and environmental outcomes. We discuss how investors can align their investments with impactful initiatives, contributing to job creation, community development, and innovation. Understanding the principles of impact investing adds a purpose-driven dimension to entrepreneurial investments.

 Celebrating Entrepreneurial Success

Acknowledging Milestones and Achievements:

Every milestone and achievement in entrepreneurship is a testament to resilience, innovation, and strategic vision. This section encourages entrepreneurs and investors to acknowledge and celebrate the successes along the entrepreneurial journey. By recognizing achievements, individuals reinforce the dedication and creativity that drive transformative business ventures.

Transitioning to New Ventures and Challenges:

As entrepreneurs achieve success in their ventures, new opportunities and challenges emerge. We discuss the process of transitioning to new ventures, whether through expansion, diversification, or addressing evolving market dynamics. Understanding the transitions between entrepreneurial ventures ensures a journey of continual growth and impact.

As we conclude this exploration of entrepreneurship and business ventures, envision yourself not just as an investor but as an architect of innovation and growth. By the end of this section, you will have gained a profound understanding of the principles and strategies that underpin successful entrepreneurship, paving the way for a journey where visionary ideas and strategic choices harmonize in perfect unity.

- Exploring Alternative Investments

In the ever-evolving landscape of investments, the pursuit of diversification and enhanced returns has led investors to explore beyond traditional asset classes. This section delves into the world of alternative investments—unconventional opportunities that span a spectrum of assets beyond stocks and bonds. Envision this journey as a quest for unique avenues that challenge conventional wisdom and redefine the boundaries of investment portfolios.

Understanding Alternative Investments

Defining Alternative Investments:

Alternative investments encompass a diverse range of assets beyond traditional stocks, bonds, and cash. This section explores the definition of alternative investments, emphasizing their distinctive characteristics, risk-return profiles, and roles within diversified portfolios. Understanding the landscape of alternative investments lays the groundwork for strategic exploration.

Rationale for Exploring Alternatives:

Investors turn to alternative investments for various reasons, including risk mitigation, return enhancement, and diversification. We discuss the rationale behind exploring alternative investments, highlighting how these assets contribute to a well-rounded and resilient investment strategy.

Understanding the motivations behind alternative investments informs strategic decision-making.

Types of Alternative Investments

Private Equity:

Private equity involves investing in privately held companies or participating in private investment funds. This section explores the nuances of private equity investments, including venture capital and buyouts. Understanding the dynamics of private equity adds a layer of potential high returns and strategic business ownership to investment portfolios

Hedge Funds:

Hedge funds are pooled investment funds that employ various strategies to generate returns. We delve into the characteristics of hedge funds, their strategies, and considerations for investors. Understanding the role of hedge funds in alternative investments offers opportunities for active management and potential diversification.

Real Assets:

Real assets, such as real estate, commodities, and natural resources, represent tangible investments with intrinsic value. This section explores how real assets contribute to alternative investment portfolios, providing avenues for inflation protection and diversification. Understanding the dynamics of real assets enriches the toolkit for constructing resilient portfolios.

Cryptocurrencies and Digital Assets:

The digital era has introduced cryptocurrencies and digital assets as alternative investment options. We discuss the characteristics of cryptocurrencies, blockchain technology, and considerations for investors navigating this evolving landscape. Understanding the potential of digital assets broadens the scope of alternative investments in the digital age.

Collectibles and Tangible Assets:

Collectables and tangible assets, including art, fine wine, and rare coins, present unique investment opportunities. This section explores the considerations involved in investing in tangible assets, including market trends and valuation. Understanding the nuances of collectable investments adds a dimension of passion and cultural appreciation to alternative portfolios.

Due Diligence and Risk Management

Conducting Due Diligence on Alternative Investments:

Thorough due diligence is paramount when exploring alternative investments. We discuss the process of researching and evaluating alternative assets, including assessing fund managers, understanding strategies, and analyzing historical performance. Understanding the principles of due diligence enhances informed decision-making in the alternative investment space.

Risk Factors in Alternative Investments:

Alternative investments come with their own set of risks, distinct from traditional assets. This section explores common risk factors associated with alternative investments, including illiquidity, market complexity, and manager risk. Understanding the specific risks in alternative investments enables investors to implement risk management strategies effectively.

Accessing Alternative Investments

Investment Vehicles for Alternatives:

Accessing alternative investments often involves specialized investment vehicles. We discuss common structures, such as limited partnerships, funds of funds, and exchange-traded funds (ETFs) focused on alternatives. Understanding the various investment vehicles provides insights into the practicalities of incorporating alternatives into investment portfolios.

Regulatory Considerations:

Regulatory considerations play a crucial role in alternative investments. This section explores the regulatory landscape governing different alternative assets and investment structures. Understanding regulatory dynamics ensures compliance and transparency in the exploration of alternative investments.

Performance Evaluation and Benchmarking

Measuring Performance in Alternative Investments:

Performance evaluation in alternative investments requires nuanced metrics. We discuss how investors assess the success of alternative assets, considering factors such as absolute returns, risk-adjusted returns, and correlation with traditional assets. Understanding alternative performance metrics enhances the ability to gauge the effectiveness of alternative strategies.

Benchmarking Alternative Investments:

Benchmarking is essential for comparing the performance of alternative investments against relevant benchmarks. This section explores the challenges and considerations involved in benchmarking alternatives, given their diverse nature. Understanding the principles of benchmarking facilitates a meaningful assessment of the relative performance of alternative assets.

Integrating Alternatives into Investment Portfolios

Asset Allocation Strategies with Alternatives:

Strategic asset allocation is a cornerstone of effective portfolio construction. We discuss how investors integrate alternative investments into their asset allocation strategies, considering factors such as risk tolerance, investment goals, and market conditions. Understanding the role of alternatives in asset allocation optimizes the diversification benefits of portfolios.

Portfolio Construction and Optimization:

Constructing and optimizing portfolios with alternative investments require a tailored approach. This section explores portfolio construction strategies, including risk parity, and considerations for optimizing alternative allocations. Understanding the dynamics of portfolio construction ensures that alternative assets complement traditional holdings for balanced risk and return profiles

Monitoring and Rebalancing Alternative Allocations:

Ongoing monitoring and periodic rebalancing are critical for maintaining optimal allocations in alternative investments. We discuss the importance of regularly assessing alternative holdings, adjusting allocations, and rebalancing portfolios. Understanding the dynamics of monitoring and rebalancing ensures that alternative investments remain aligned with overall investment objectives.

Ethical and Sustainable Alternatives

Ethical and Sustainable Investment Options:

Investors increasingly seek ethical and sustainable alternatives. This section explores how alternative investments can align with environmental, social, and governance (ESG) principles. Understanding the landscape of ethical alternatives empowers investors to make choices that resonate with their values and sustainability goals.

Impact Investing in Alternative Assets:

Beyond financial returns, impact investing in alternative assets aims to generate positive social and environmental outcomes. We discuss how investors can align their alternative investments with impactful initiatives, contributing to sustainability and social responsibility. Understanding the principles of impact investing in alternatives adds a purpose-driven dimension to investment portfolios.

Celebrating the Diversity of Alternative Investments

Acknowledging the Unique Contributions of Alternatives:

Every alternative investment brings a unique set of characteristics to a portfolio. This section encourages investors to acknowledge and appreciate the diversity within their alternative holdings. By recognizing the unique contributions of alternatives, investors reinforce a well-rounded and innovative approach to wealth-building.

Transitioning to Advanced Alternative Strategies:

As investors gain experience, they may explore advanced alternative strategies, including managed futures, derivatives, or niche opportunities. Understanding the possibilities of advanced alternative strategies positions investors to adapt their approach as their financial knowledge and goals evolve.

As we conclude this exploration of alternative investments, envision yourself not just as an investor but as an explorer charting new territories within the investment landscape. By the end of this section, you will have gained a profound understanding of the principles and strategies that underpin the successful exploration of alternative investments, paving the way for a journey where innovation, diversity, and strategic choices harmonize in perfect unity.

CHAPTER 5:
CRUSHING DEBT AND SUPERCHARGING YOUR WEALTH

In the intricate tapestry of personal finance, the weight of debt can cast a looming shadow on financial aspirations. Yet, within the challenge of crushing debt lies a transformative opportunity to reclaim control, reshape financial habits, and pave the way for supercharging wealth. This chapter embarks on a journey of financial empowerment, guiding you through strategic approaches to liberate yourself from the shackles of debt and set the stage for unparalleled wealth creation.

Unveiling the Debt Dilemma

Understanding the Impact of Debt:

Debt, when left unaddressed, can become a formidable barrier to financial freedom. This section explores the various forms of debt, from credit cards to loans, and delves into the profound impact it can have on your financial health. Understanding the nuances of the debt dilemma is the first step towards formulating a comprehensive strategy for liberation.

The Psychological Burden of Debt:

Beyond the financial implications, debt often exerts a significant psychological toll. We discuss how the stress and anxiety associated with debt can impact overall well-being and decision-making. Understanding the psychological dimensions of debt empowers you to cultivate a mindset conducive to breaking free from its grip.

Crafting Your Debt Repayment Strategy

Assessing and Prioritizing Debt:

Not all debts are created equal. This section guides you through the process of assessing and prioritizing your debts based on factors such as interest rates, terms, and overall financial impact. Understanding how to strategically approach different types of debt lays the groundwork for an efficient repayment plan.

Creating a Realistic Debt Repayment Plan:

A well-crafted debt repayment plan is your roadmap to financial liberation. We explore the principles of creating a realistic plan that aligns with your income, expenses, and financial goals. Understanding the dynamics of a personalized debt repayment strategy sets the stage for steady progress towards a debt-free future.

Supercharging Wealth Amidst Debt Repayment

Simultaneous Wealth Building and Debt Repayment:

Contrary to conventional wisdom, wealth building and debt repayment can coexist. This section introduces the concept of simultaneous wealth building, exploring how strategic financial decisions can accelerate your journey to both debt freedom and wealth accumulation. Understanding the synergy between these objectives unlocks the potential for financial supercharging.

Leveraging Debt as a Tool for Wealth Creation:

Debt, when used strategically, can become a powerful tool for wealth creation. We discuss how leveraging debt for investments, such as real estate or education, can amplify returns and pave the way for long-term prosperity. Understanding how to harness debt as a constructive force transforms your financial approach.

Tackling High-Interest Debt

Strategies for Tackling Credit Card Debt:

High-interest credit card debt often poses a significant challenge. This section unveils strategic approaches to tackle credit card debt, including consolidation, negotiation, and systematic repayment. Understanding the intricacies of handling high-interest debt empowers you to reclaim control over your financial destiny.

Navigating Student Loans and Educational Debt:

Student loans and educational debt can linger long after graduation. We discuss practical strategies for navigating student loans, including repayment plans, refinancing options, and leveraging income-driven approaches. Understanding the nuances of educational debt equips you to balance debt repayment with ongoing financial goals.

Lifestyle Adjustments for Financial Liberation

Budgeting for Liberation:

Budgeting becomes a crucial ally in the quest for financial liberation. This section explores the principles of budgeting for debt repayment, emphasizing the importance of disciplined spending and strategic allocation of resources. Understanding how to craft a budget tailored to your financial goals creates a solid foundation for sustained progress.

Embracing Frugality and Smart Spending:

The journey towards financial freedom often involves a mindset shift towards frugality and smart spending. We discuss how embracing a frugal lifestyle can accelerate debt repayment and amplify wealth-building efforts. Understanding the principles of frugality empowers you to make intentional choices that align with your financial objectives.

Building Financial Resilience

Emergency Funds and Financial Cushions:

Financial resilience is anchored in preparedness. This section explores the importance of emergency funds and financial cushions, providing a safety net for unexpected expenses and preventing the accumulation of high-interest debt. Understanding the role of financial reserves enhances your ability to navigate financial challenges with confidence.

Insurance as a Protective Shield:

Insurance acts as a protective shield against unforeseen events that could otherwise lead to financial setbacks. We discuss the role of insurance in mitigating risks and safeguarding your financial well-being. Understanding how insurance contributes to financial resilience adds layers of protection to your overall financial strategy.

The Psychology of Debt Liberation

Celebrating Milestones and Progress:

Every milestone in the journey towards debt liberation is a victory to be celebrated. This section encourages you to acknowledge and appreciate the progress you make along the way. By recognizing milestones, you reinforce a positive mindset that propels you towards your ultimate financial goals.

Cultivating Financial Confidence and Freedom:

Financial confidence is a byproduct of strategic decision-making and progress towards financial goals. We explore how cultivating financial confidence contributes to a sense of freedom and empowerment. Understanding the dynamics of financial confidence positions you to embrace a future characterized by financial autonomy.

Your Personalized Path to Wealth

Crafting a Wealth-Building Blueprint:

As you embark on the path of debt liberation, crafting a personalized wealth-building blueprint becomes essential. This section guides you through the process of setting financial goals, making strategic investment decisions, and cultivating a mindset of abundance. Understanding how to create a wealth-building blueprint transforms your financial journey into a narrative of empowerment and prosperity.

Transitioning to Advanced Wealth-Building Strategies:

As your financial journey evolves, you may explore advanced wealth-building strategies, such as investment diversification, business ventures, or alternative investments. We discuss how to transition to advanced strategies, and understanding the intricacies of elevating your wealth-building approach.

In the chapters that follow, prepare to witness the transformation of financial challenges into stepping stones towards wealth supercharging. By the end of this chapter, you will have gained a profound understanding of the principles and strategies that underpin the art of crushing debt and unlocking the doors to unparalleled wealth creation. Your journey to financial liberation and prosperity starts here.

- Eliminating Debt Efficiently

Debt can often feel like a heavy burden, casting a shadow over your financial well-being and long-term goals. However, with a strategic and disciplined approach, you can efficiently eliminate debt, freeing yourself from its constraints and paving the way for a brighter financial future. This section explores a comprehensive process for efficiently tackling and eliminating various types of debt.

1. Assessment and Organization:

- **Compile a Debt Inventory:** Start by creating a comprehensive list of all your debts. Include details such as the type of debt (credit cards, loans, mortgages), outstanding balances, interest rates, and minimum monthly payments.

- **Organize by Priority:** Prioritize debts based on interest rates, with high-interest debts taking precedence. Consider factors such as the size of the debt and any potential repercussions for non-payment.

2. Create a Realistic Budget:

- **Track Income and Expenses:** Develop a detailed budget that outlines your monthly income and all expenditures. This helps identify areas where you can cut back to allocate more funds towards debt repayment.

- **Allocate Extra Funds:** Determine how much extra money you can allocate towards debt repayment each month. This may involve adjusting spending habits or identifying additional sources of income.

3. **Emergency Fund Establishment:**

- **Create a Financial Cushion:** Build an emergency fund to cover unexpected expenses. This prevents relying on credit cards or loans for unforeseen circumstances, reducing the risk of accumulating more debt during the repayment process.

4. **Negotiation and Consolidation:**

- **Negotiate Interest Rates:** Reach out to creditors to negotiate lower interest rates, especially on credit cards. A lower rate can significantly reduce the total amount paid over time.

   - **Consider Consolidation:** Explore debt consolidation options, such as transferring high-interest credit card balances to a single, lower-interest loan. Consolidation simplifies repayment and potentially lowers interest costs.

5. Debt Snowball or Avalanche Method:

   - **Snowball Method:** Start by paying off the smallest debt first while maintaining minimum payments on others. Once the smallest debt is cleared, roll the payment into the next smallest debt.

   - **Avalanche Method:** Prioritize debts based on interest rates, focusing on the highest interest rate first. Allocate extra funds to the highest-rate debt while making minimum payments on others. Once paid off, move to the next highest interest rate.

6. Increase Income Streams:

- **Side Hustles and Additional Work:** Explore opportunities for side hustles or part-time work to supplement your income. Allocate the additional income exclusively towards debt repayment.

- **Sell Unnecessary Assets:** Consider selling unused or unnecessary possessions to generate extra funds for debt elimination.

7. Windfall Allocation:

- **Direct Windfalls to Debt:** If you receive unexpected windfalls such as tax refunds, bonuses, or gifts, allocate a significant portion directly to debt repayment.

- **Avoid Lifestyle Inflation:** Resist the urge to increase spending when experiencing financial windfalls, and instead, redirect these funds towards debt reduction.

8. Financial Counseling:

- **Seek Professional Guidance:** Consider consulting a financial counsellor or advisor to get personalized advice on debt management. They can provide insights into debt consolidation, negotiation strategies, and budget optimization.

9. **Behavioral Adjustments:**

- **Identify Spending Triggers:** Understand the emotional and psychological triggers that lead to excessive spending. Addressing these triggers can prevent the future accumulation of debt.

- **Cultivate Financial Discipline:** Develop habits that reinforce financial discipline, such as avoiding impulsive purchases and adhering strictly to the budget.

10. **Regular Monitoring and Adjustments:**

- **Track Progress:** Regularly monitor your debt repayment progress. Celebrate milestones and stay motivated by visualizing the reduction in outstanding balances.

- **Adjust Strategies:** If necessary, reassess your debt elimination strategies. Consider adjustments based on changes in income, expenses, or unexpected financial developments.

11. Educational Resources:

- **Financial Literacy Education:** Invest time in learning about financial literacy and debt management. Various online resources, books, and workshops offer valuable insights into efficient debt-elimination strategies.

- **Debt Repayment Apps:** Explore the use of debt repayment apps that provide tools, calculators, and personalized plans to streamline the process.

12. Continuous Improvement:

- **Apply Learnings:** As you progress in debt elimination, apply lessons learned to your overall financial management. Cultivate a mindset of continuous improvement for sustained financial well-being.

- **Prevent Recurrence:** Implement measures to prevent a recurrence of debt accumulation, such as maintaining an emergency fund and practicing prudent financial habits.

Efficiently eliminating debt is a journey that requires commitment, discipline, and strategic decision-making. By following this comprehensive process, you can not only break free from the chains of debt but also lay the foundation for a more secure and prosperous financial future. As you embark on this path, envision each debt payment as a step closer to financial liberation and the supercharging of your wealth.

- Creating a Debt Repayment Plan

A structured and well-thought-out debt repayment plan is instrumental in regaining financial control and paving the way towards a debt-free future. Here's a comprehensive guide to creating an effective debt repayment plan:

1. **Assess Your Debt Inventory:**

  - **Compile a Detailed List:** Create a comprehensive inventory of all your debts. Include information such as the type of debt, outstanding balance, interest rate, minimum monthly payment, and due dates.

  - **Categorize Debts:** Group debts into categories such as high-interest credit cards, student loans, and personal loans. This categorization sets the stage for prioritization.

2. **Prioritize Debts:**

  - **Identify High-Interest Debts:** Prioritize debts with the highest interest rates to minimize overall interest payments. These are typically credit card debts or loans with variable interest rates.

  - **Consider Outstanding Balances:** While interest rates are crucial, also consider the outstanding balances. Some may opt for the "Debt Snowball" method, tackling smaller debts first for psychological wins.

3. Determine Monthly Repayment Capacity:

- **Evaluate Your Budget:** Assess your monthly income and expenses to determine the amount you can allocate towards debt repayment.

- **Allocate Extra Funds:** Identify areas where you can cut back on discretionary spending to allocate extra funds to debt repayment.

4. Emergency Fund Establishment:

- **Set Up an Emergency Fund:** Before aggressive debt repayment, establish a small emergency fund to cover unexpected expenses. This prevents the need to accumulate more debt in case of emergencies.

5. Choose a Repayment Strategy:

- **Debt Snowball Method:** Start by paying off the smallest debt first, then roll the payment into the next smallest debt. This method provides quick wins and motivation.

- **Debt Avalanche Method:** Prioritize debts based on interest rates, focusing on the highest rate first. This method minimizes overall interest payments.

6. Negotiate Interest Rates:

- **Contact Creditors:** Reach out to creditors to negotiate lower interest rates, especially on credit cards. Lower rates reduce the overall cost of debt.

- **Consider Balance Transfers:** Explore balance transfer options for credit cards to consolidate high-interest debts onto a card with a lower interest rate.

7. Consolidation Consideration:

- **Debt Consolidation Loan:** Explore the option of a debt consolidation loan to combine multiple debts into a single, more manageable payment with a potentially lower interest rate.

- **Student Loan Consolidation:** For those with multiple student loans, investigate federal or private student loan consolidation options.

8. **Create a Repayment Schedule:**

- **Monthly Payment Plan:** Outline a detailed monthly payment plan that includes the amount allocated to each debt.

- **Due Dates**: Ensure your payments align with due dates to avoid late fees. Set up automatic payments when possible to streamline the process.

9. **Increase Income Streams:**

- **Side Hustles or Part-Time Work:** Explore opportunities for additional income through side hustles or part-time work.

- **Sell Unnecessary Items:** Sell items you no longer need to generate extra funds for debt repayment.

10. **Windfall Allocation:**

- **Direct Windfalls to Debt:** Allocate unexpected windfalls, such as tax refunds or bonuses, directly to debt repayment.

- **Avoid Lifestyle Inflation:** Resist the temptation to increase spending when experiencing financial windfalls.

11. Continuous Monitoring and Adjustments:

- **Regularly Assess Progress:** Periodically review your debt repayment plan to track progress. Celebrate milestones to stay motivated.

- **Adjust Strategies:** If circumstances change, reassess your plan and make adjustments accordingly.

12. Seek Professional Guidance:

- **Financial Counseling:** Consider seeking advice from financial counsellors or debt management professionals. They can provide personalized strategies and negotiation assistance.

13. Build Long-Term Financial Habits:

- **Budgeting:** Cultivate a habit of budgeting to manage expenses and ensure consistent debt repayment.

- Emergency Fund Maintenance: Once debts are paid off, continue building your emergency fund to prevent future reliance on credit in emergencies.

14. **Celebrate Achievements:**

- Acknowledge Milestones: Celebrate each debt that you successfully eliminate. Acknowledge the progress made on your journey to financial freedom.

- Maintain Motivation: Use celebrations as motivation to stay committed to your debt repayment plan.

Creating a debt repayment plan is not only about the financial aspects but also about building discipline and resilience. By following these steps and staying committed to your plan, you'll find yourself steadily moving towards a debt-free and financially secure future. As you embark on this journey, envision each payment as a step closer to your ultimate financial goals.

- Prioritizing High-Interest Debts

Prioritizing high-interest debts is a crucial step in any effective debt repayment strategy. By addressing debts with the highest interest rates first, you can minimize the overall cost of borrowing and accelerate your journey toward financial freedom. Here's a comprehensive guide on how to strategically prioritize high-interest debts:

1. **Compile a Detailed Debt Inventory:**

   - **List All Debts:** Create a comprehensive list of all your debts, including credit cards, personal loans, and any other outstanding balances.

   - **Gather Key Information:** Note the outstanding balances, interest rates, minimum monthly payments, and due dates for each debt.

2. **Identify High-Interest Debts:**

- **Sort by Interest Rates:** Organize your debts based on their interest rates, from highest to lowest.

- **Highlight High-Interest Debts:** Identify the debts with the highest interest rates. These are the ones that will cost you the most over time.

3. Consider Outstanding Balances:

- **Evaluate Debt Sizes:** While interest rates are crucial, also consider the outstanding balances. Assess whether there are smaller debts with higher interest rates that you can prioritize for quicker wins.

4. Calculate the Cost of High-Interest Debts:

- **Use a Debt Calculator:** Utilize online debt calculators to estimate the total cost of high-interest debts over time.

- **Understand the Impact:** Seeing the long-term impact of high interest rates can serve as motivation to prioritize and eliminate these debts sooner.

5. Assess Your Monthly Repayment Capacity:

- **Review Your Budget:** Evaluate your monthly income and expenses to determine how much you can allocate toward debt repayment.

- **Identify Extra Funds:** Look for areas where you can cut back on discretionary spending to free up additional funds for debt repayment.

6. Emergency Fund Consideration:

- **Establish an Emergency Fund:** Before aggressively tackling high-interest debts, ensure you have a small emergency fund to cover unexpected expenses. This prevents reliance on credit cards in emergencies.

7. Negotiate Interest Rates:

- **Contact Creditors:** Reach out to creditors to negotiate lower interest rates, especially for credit cards. A reduction in interest rates directly impacts the overall cost of debt.

8. **Consider Balance Transfers or Debt Consolidation:**

   - **Explore Balance Transfers:** Investigate the possibility of transferring high-interest credit card balances to cards with lower interest rates.

   - **Debt Consolidation:** Consider consolidating multiple high-interest debts into a single, more manageable loan with a lower interest rate.

9. **Allocate Extra Funds to High-Interest Debts:**

   - **Prioritize Payments:** Allocate any extra funds or windfalls directly to the high-interest debts.

   - **Avoid Minimum Payment Traps:** While making minimum payments on other debts, focus on aggressively paying down the principal of high-interest debts.

10. **Evaluate the Impact on Credit Score:**

   - **Understand Credit Score Dynamics:** Prioritizing high-interest debts may lead to faster improvements in your credit score, as reducing outstanding balances positively affects credit utilization ratios.

- **Monitor Credit Reports:** Regularly check your credit reports to ensure that creditors accurately reflect your efforts in paying down high-interest debts.

11. Maintain Minimum Payments on Other Debts:

- **Prevent Penalties:** Continue making at least the minimum payments on all other debts to avoid penalties and maintain a positive credit history.

- **Strategically Allocate Funds:** Distribute remaining funds strategically, focusing on high-interest debts while fulfilling minimum obligations.

12. Track Progress and Celebrate Milestones:

- **Use Debt Tracking Tools:** Employ debt tracking tools to monitor progress. Many apps and online platforms provide visual representations of debt reduction.

- **Celebrate Achievements:** Acknowledge and celebrate each milestone as you successfully eliminate high-interest debts. This positive reinforcement boosts motivation.

13. **Reassess and Adjust as Needed:**

- **Regularly Reevaluate:** Periodically reassess your financial situation, income, and expenses. Adjust your prioritization strategy as needed.

- **Consider Windfalls:** Allocate unexpected windfalls directly to high-interest debts to expedite repayment.

14. **Seek Professional Advice:**

- **Financial Counseling:** If needed, consider seeking advice from financial counsellors or advisors. They can provide insights into negotiation strategies and debt management.

15. **Build Long-Term Financial Habits:**

- **Budgeting and Emergency Funds:** Cultivate habits of budgeting and maintaining emergency funds even after high-interest debts are paid off.

- **Avoiding Future High-Interest Debt:** Learn from the experience and adopt financial practices that prevent the accumulation of high-interest debts in the future.

Prioritizing high-interest debts requires a strategic and disciplined approach. By following these steps, you'll not only minimize the financial impact of high interest rates but also pave the way for a more secure and prosperous financial future. As you work through the process, envision each payment as a step closer to eliminating high-interest debts and achieving financial freedom.

- Negotiating Favorable Terms with Creditors

Negotiating with creditors is a proactive and strategic approach to managing debt, potentially leading to more manageable terms and reduced financial strain. Here's a comprehensive guide on how to negotiate favorable terms with creditors:

1. Understand Your Financial Situation:

- **Gather Financial Information:** Compile accurate information about your income, expenses, and outstanding debts.

- **Assess Your Ability to Repay:** Understand your financial capacity to determine realistic and sustainable repayment terms.

2. Prioritize Your Debts:

- **Identify High-Priority Debts:** Determine which debts need immediate attention based on factors like interest rates, penalties, and potential legal consequences.

- **Create a Repayment Plan:** Develop a clear plan outlining how you intend to address each debt, considering your negotiation goals.

3. Know Your Rights:

- Understand Consumer Protection Laws:
Familiarize yourself with relevant consumer protection laws, including the Fair Debt Collection Practices Act (FDCPA) and other regulations that safeguard your rights.

- Verify Debt Information: Ensure the accuracy of the debt information provided by creditors and collection agencies.

4. Prepare a Budget Proposal:

- Detail Your Financial Situation: Present a comprehensive overview of your income, expenses, and outstanding debts.

- Propose Realistic Payments: Based on your financial assessment, propose a realistic repayment plan that you can sustain. Clearly articulate why these terms are feasible for you.

5. Initiate Contact with Creditors:

- Communicate Early: Reach out to creditors as soon as you anticipate financial challenges. Early communication demonstrates responsibility and a willingness to address the issue.

 - **Use Written Communication:** Whenever possible, communicate in writing to create a documented record of your interactions.

 6. **Be Honest and Transparent:**

 - **Explain Your Situation:** communicate the circumstances that led to your financial challenges. Provide context, such as job loss, medical issues, or other unexpected events.

 - **Highlight Your Willingness to Pay:** Emphasize your commitment to resolving the debt and your intent to work collaboratively with the creditor.

 7. **Negotiate Interest Rates:**

 - **Research Market Rates:** Familiarize yourself with current interest rates in the market for similar financial products.

- **Propose Lower Rates:** Negotiate for reduced interest rates on outstanding balances, especially if you have a good payment history.

8. Explore Debt Settlement Options:

- **Offer Lump-Sum Payments:** If possible, propose a lump-sum payment to settle the debt for less than the total owed.

- **Negotiate a Percentage:** Discuss a percentage of the total debt that you can afford to pay immediately.

9. Request Fee Waivers and Penalties:

- **Ask for Waived Fees:** Inquire about the possibility of having late fees, over-limit fees, or other penalties waived.

- **Negotiate Lower Penalties:** If applicable, negotiate for reduced penalties, especially those associated with missed payments.

10. Seek Temporary Relief:

- Request Temporary Forbearance: In times of financial distress, inquire about temporary forbearance or deferment options.

- Propose a Temporary Payment Reduction: If a short-term reduction in payments would help, propose this as a temporary solution.

11. Consider Professional Mediation:

- Engage Credit Counseling Agencies: Enlist the services of reputable credit counselling agencies that can act as intermediaries between you and creditors.

- Explore Debt Settlement Companies: Evaluate the pros and cons of working with debt settlement companies if negotiations become challenging.

12. Document Agreements in Writing:

- Create Written Agreements: Once terms are agreed upon, ensure that the new terms, including any changes to interest rates or payment schedules, are documented in writing.

- **Retain Copies of Correspondence:** Keep copies of all written correspondence and agreements for your records.

13. Follow Up Regularly:

- **Check Progress:** Regularly follow up with creditors to ensure that agreed-upon terms are being implemented.

- **Provide Updates:** If there are changes in your financial situation, communicate these changes promptly to maintain transparency.

14. Seek Legal Advice if Necessary:

- **Consult with an Attorney:** If negotiations become challenging or if you face potential legal consequences, seek advice from a consumer protection attorney.

- **Know Your Rights:** Understand your rights and legal protections against unfair debt collection practices.

15. **Rebuild Your Credit:**

- **Implement Positive Financial Habits:** As you make payments and settle debts, focus on rebuilding your credit by implementing positive financial habits.

- **Monitor Your Credit Report:** Regularly check your credit report to ensure that accurate information is reflected, and disputed items are resolved.

Negotiating with creditors requires preparation, honesty, and a proactive approach. By demonstrating your commitment to resolving the debt and proposing realistic terms, you increase the likelihood of reaching agreements that are favorable to both parties. As you navigate this process, keep in mind that clear communication and a willingness to collaborate can lead to more manageable debt repayment terms.

- Turning Debt into Wealth-Building Opportunities

While debt is typically viewed as a financial burden, it can be transformed into a stepping stone for wealth-building when approached strategically. Here's a comprehensive guide on turning debt into wealth-building opportunities:

1. **Assess Your Debt Landscape:**

   - **Create a Debt Inventory:** List all your debts, including outstanding balances, interest rates, and monthly payments.

   - **Categorize Debts:** Differentiate between high-interest consumer debts (credit cards) and potentially strategic debts (mortgage, student loans).

2. **Prioritize Strategic Debts:**

   - Identify Investment-Friendly Debts: Prioritize debts that have the potential to yield future returns or enhance your financial situation (e.g., student loans for education, mortgage for real estate).

   - Prioritize High-Interest Debts: Tackle high-interest consumer debts to minimize interest payments.

3. Leverage Low-Interest Debt for Investments:

   - Evaluate Low-Interest Options: If you have access to low-interest debt (e.g., low-interest loans, lines of credit), consider using it strategically for investments with higher potential returns.

   - Invest in Income-Generating Assets: Direct funds towards investments that generate passive income, such as real estate, dividend-paying stocks, or business ventures.

4. Debt Recycling Strategies:

   - Reinvest Loan Repayments: As you pay down one debt, consider reinvesting those freed-up funds into new wealth-building opportunities.

- **Use Home Equity Wisely:** If you have equity in your home, consider strategic uses like home renovations that can increase property value.

5. **Consolidate and Refinance:**

- **Explore Consolidation Options:** Consolidate multiple high-interest debts into a single loan with a lower interest rate.

- **Refinance High-Interest Loans:** Refinance loans, such as student loans or personal loans, to secure more favorable terms.

6. **Invest in Education and Skill Development:**

- **Strategic Use of Student Loans:** If you have student loans, consider them as an investment in your education and future earning potential.

- **Continuous Learning:** Invest in courses or certifications that enhance your skills and increase your marketability, potentially leading to higher income.

7. **Real Estate as a Wealth-Building Tool:**

- **Strategic Real Estate Investments:** Use mortgage debt strategically for real estate investments that have the potential for appreciation or rental income.

- **Homeownership Benefits:** Leverage the long-term wealth-building benefits of homeownership.

8. **Invest in Marketable Skills:**

- **Skill-Based Investments:** Invest in acquiring skills that are in demand in the job market or freelancing platforms.

- **Freelancing Opportunities:** Turn these skills into freelancing opportunities, creating additional income streams.

9. **Entrepreneurial Ventures:**

- **Strategic Business Debt:** If considering entrepreneurship, strategically use business loans for ventures with growth potential.

- **Debt for Expansion:** Consider business expansion loans for scaling operations and increasing revenue.

10. **Create a Debt Repayment Plan:**

- **Structured Repayment:** Develop a clear plan to systematically pay down high-interest debts.

- **Allocate Windfalls:** Use unexpected windfalls or bonuses to make substantial payments toward high-interest debts.

11. **Emergency Fund and Financial Security:**

- **Prioritize Financial Security:** Use a portion of wealth-building returns to establish or strengthen your emergency fund.

- **Protection Against Debt Accumulation:** A robust emergency fund prevents reliance on credit in times of unexpected expenses.

12. Tax-Efficient Strategies:

- **Tax-Advantaged Investments:** Explore tax-efficient investment options, such as retirement accounts, to optimize returns.

- **Utilize Tax Deductions:** Certain types of debt, like mortgage interest, may offer tax deductions, enhancing your overall financial strategy.

13. Monitor and Adjust Strategies:

- **Regular Financial Checkups:** Periodically review your debt, investments, and financial goals.

- **Adjust Strategies as Needed:** If circumstances change or new opportunities arise, be flexible in adjusting your wealth-building strategies.

14. Diversify Your Investments:

- **Spread Investments Across Assets:** Diversify your investments across different asset classes to mitigate risk.

- **Balanced Portfolio:** Aim for a balanced portfolio that aligns with your risk tolerance and financial goals.

15. **Continuous Learning and Adaptation:**

- **Stay Financially Informed:** Keep abreast of financial trends, investment opportunities, and debt management strategies.

- **Adapt to Changing Circumstances:** Be adaptable in your approach, especially in response to changes in the economic landscape or personal circumstances.

16. **Cultivate a Wealth-Building Mindset:**

- **Positive Financial Habits:** Cultivate positive financial habits that support wealth-building goals.

- **Long-Term Perspective:** Adopt a long-term perspective, understanding that the journey from debt to wealth is a gradual and strategic process.

By reframing your approach to debt and viewing it as a tool for strategic wealth-building, you can harness its potential to create lasting financial prosperity. This transformation involves careful planning, prioritization, and a commitment to leveraging debt as a stepping stone toward your broader financial goals.

- Leveraging Debt for Strategic Investments

Leveraging debt for strategic investments involves using borrowed funds to potentially generate higher returns and accelerate wealth-building. Here's a detailed guide on how to navigate this process responsibly and strategically:

1. **Understand the Concept of Leverage:**

   - **Definition:** Leverage involves using borrowed capital to increase the potential return on an investment.

- **Risk and Reward:** While leverage can amplify returns, it also magnifies risks. Understanding this balance is crucial.

2. Assess Your Financial Situation:

- **Financial Health:** Evaluate your overall financial health, including income, expenses, and existing debts.

- **Risk Tolerance:** Assess your risk tolerance and comfort level with taking on additional debt for investments.

3. Distinguish Between Good and Bad Debt:

- **Good Debt:** Identify debts that can potentially yield positive returns, such as mortgage debt for real estate or student loans for education.

- **Bad Debt:** Distinguish high-interest consumer debts (credit cards, payday loans) as potentially detrimental to wealth-building.

4. Identify Investment Opportunities:

- **Research and Due Diligence:** Conduct thorough research on potential investments. This could include real estate, stocks, bonds, or starting a business.

- **Risk and Return Analysis:** Evaluate the risk and return profile of each investment opportunity.

5. Explore Low-Interest Borrowing Options:

- **Low-Interest Loans:** Look for borrowing options with favorable interest rates, such as personal loans, lines of credit, or mortgages with low rates.

- **Balance Transfer Offers:** Consider balance transfer offers on credit cards with low introductory rates for short-term financing.

6. Calculate Debt Serviceability:

- **Evaluate Monthly Payments:** Calculate the monthly debt payments required for the borrowed funds.

- **Ensure Affordability:** Confirm that you can comfortably service the debt without compromising your financial stability.

7. Create a Strategic Investment Plan:

- **Define Investment Goals:** Clearly outline your investment goals, whether it's long-term capital appreciation, generating passive income, or building a business.

- **Allocate Funds Strategically:** Determine how much-borrowed capital to allocate to each investment, considering potential returns and risks.

8. Diversify Investments:

- **Spread Risk:** Diversify your investments across different asset classes to spread risk.

- **Balanced Portfolio:** Aim for a balanced portfolio that aligns with your financial objectives and risk tolerance.

9. Utilize Real Estate as a Leveraging Tool:

- **Mortgage Leverage:** Consider using mortgage loans to finance real estate investments. The property itself serves as collateral.

- **Home Equity Loans:** Leverage the equity in your existing property for additional real estate investments.

10. Explore Investment Loans:

- **Margin Loans for Stocks:** Consider margin loans for investing in stocks, where the investment portfolio acts as collateral.

- **Business Loans for Entrepreneurship:** If starting or expanding a business, explore business loans for strategic growth.

11. Evaluate Tax Implications:

- **Tax-Deductible Interest:** Some types of investment-related debt may offer tax-deductible interest, providing potential tax advantages.

- **Consult Tax Professionals:** Seek advice from tax professionals to understand the tax implications of leveraging debt for specific investments.

12. Establish an Emergency Fund:

- **Financial Safety Net:** Maintain a robust emergency fund to cover unexpected expenses and ensure financial stability.

- **Risk Mitigation:** Having an emergency fund reduces the risk of financial distress in case investments face temporary setbacks.

13. Monitor and Adjust Strategies:

- **Regular Financial Reviews:** Periodically review the performance of your investments and assess whether the leverage is contributing to your wealth-building goals.

- **Adjust as Needed:** If market conditions change or investment performance deviates from expectations, be willing to adjust your strategy.

14. Retain a Long-Term Perspective:

- **Patience in Wealth-Building:** Understand that wealth-building is a long-term endeavor. Be patient and resist the urge to make impulsive decisions based on short-term market fluctuations.

15. Continuous Learning:

- **Stay Informed:** Keep abreast of market trends, investment opportunities, and changes in economic conditions.

- **Educate Yourself:** Continuously educate yourself on financial markets, investment strategies, and the evolving landscape.

16. Risk Management:

- **Risk Mitigation Strategies:** Implement risk management strategies, such as setting stop-loss limits and diversifying investments, to mitigate potential downsides.

- **Insurance Coverage:** Ensure you have adequate insurance coverage to protect against unforeseen events that could impact your investments.

17. **Professional Advice:**

- **Consult Financial Advisors:** Seek advice from financial advisors who can provide personalized guidance based on your financial goals and risk tolerance.

- **Legal and Tax Consultation:** Before entering complex investment arrangements, consult legal and tax professionals to understand potential legal and tax implications.

Leveraging debt for strategic investments can be a powerful tool for wealth-building, but it requires careful planning, risk assessment, and ongoing management. When executed prudently, leveraging debt can potentially accelerate the growth of your portfolio and contribute to long-term financial success.

- Using Credit Wisely for Financial Growth

Credit can be a valuable tool when used wisely, catalyzing financial growth and opportunities. Here's a comprehensive guide on how to navigate the process of using credit responsibly for financial advancement:

1. **Understand Your Credit Profile:**

   - **Check Your Credit Report:** Regularly obtain and review your credit report from major credit bureaus (Equifax, Experian, TransUnion).

   - **Monitor Your Credit Score:** Keep track of your credit score, understanding how it's calculated and the factors influencing it.

2. **Differentiate Between Good and Bad Debt:**

   - **Good Debt:** Recognize debts that have the potential for positive returns, such as mortgage debt, student loans, or business loans for strategic investments.

- **Bad Debt:** Identify high-interest, non-essential debts like credit card debt, which can hinder financial growth.

3. Build and Maintain a Positive Credit History:

- **Timely Payments:** Pay all bills, loans, and credit card balances on time to establish and maintain a positive payment history.

- **Diversify Credit Types:** Having a mix of credit types (credit cards, instalment loans) contributes positively to your credit score.

4. Establish an Emergency Fund:

- **Financial Safety Net:** Before utilizing credit for growth, ensure you have a robust emergency fund to cover unexpected expenses.

- **Prevent Reliance on Credit:** Having an emergency fund reduces the need to rely on credit for unforeseen circumstances.

5. Strategically Use Credit Cards:

- **Credit Card Benefits:** Utilize credit cards for convenience, rewards, and building credit.

- **Pay in Full Monthly:** Whenever possible, pay your credit card balance in full each month to avoid interest charges.

6. Credit Card Rewards and Cash Back:

- **Maximize Rewards:** Choose credit cards with rewards programs aligned with your spending habits. Maximize rewards for travel, cash back, or other benefits.

- **Redeem Strategically:** Redeem rewards in a way that enhances your financial situation, such as using cash back to pay down balances.

7. Strategic Use of Low-Interest Loans:

- **Low-Interest Personal Loans:** Consider low-interest personal loans for strategic purposes, such as debt consolidation or home improvements.

- **Balance Transfers:** Explore balance transfer options for high-interest debts, consolidating them onto a card with a lower interest rate.

8. Invest in Marketable Skills:

- **Education Loans:** Strategically use education loans for acquiring skills and education that enhance your earning potential.

- **Return on Investment (ROI):** Evaluate the potential return on investment in terms of increased income and career opportunities.

9. Leverage Credit for Real Estate Investments:

- **Mortgage Loans:** Use mortgage loans strategically for real estate investments. Homeownership can be a wealth-building opportunity.

- **Home Equity Loans:** Leverage home equity for renovations or additional real estate investments.

10. Business Credit for Entrepreneurship:

- **Business Loans:** Consider business loans for entrepreneurial ventures, expansion, or working capital.

- **Business Credit Lines:** Establish and responsibly use business credit lines to support ongoing operations.

11. Monitor Credit Utilization:

- **Maintain Low Credit Utilization:** Keep credit card balances low relative to credit limits to positively impact your credit score.

- **Avoid Maxing Out Credit:** Avoid maxing out credit cards, as high credit utilization can negatively affect your credit score.

12. Manage Debt-to-Income Ratio:

- **Calculate Debt-to-Income Ratio:** Assess your debt-to-income ratio to ensure that you're not overextended financially.

- **Strive for Balance:** Aim for a balance where your debt obligations are manageable relative to your income.

13. **Regularly Review and Adjust Credit Strategies:**

- **Periodic Credit Assessments:** Periodically review your credit strategies in light of changing financial goals or economic conditions.

- **Adjust as Needed:** Be willing to adjust your credit usage based on your financial situation and objectives.

14. **Avoid Impulse Spending:**

- **Mindful Purchases:** Practice mindful spending to avoid accumulating unnecessary debt.

- **Budgeting:** Implement a budget to track and control your expenses, ensuring responsible credit use.

15. Emergency Use of Credit:

- **Last Resort:** Use credit as a last resort for genuine emergencies, emphasizing the importance of maintaining financial resilience.

- **Have a Repayment Plan:** If using credit for emergencies, have a clear plan for repaying the borrowed funds.

16. Financial Education and Counseling:

- **Continuous Learning:** Stay informed about credit management, financial literacy, and changes in the credit landscape.

- **Professional Advice:** Seek advice from financial counsellors or advisors for personalized guidance on credit management strategies.

17. **Protect Against Identity Theft:**

- **Monitor Accounts:** Regularly monitor your financial accounts for any unauthorized activity.

- **Use Security Measures:** Employ security measures, such as strong passwords and two-factor authentication, to protect against identity theft.

18. **Build a Positive Credit Legacy:**

- **Teach Responsible Credit Use:** Instill responsible credit habits in future generations by sharing knowledge about credit management with family members.

- **Generational Financial Health:** Contribute to generational financial health by leaving a positive credit legacy.

19. **Seek Professional Advice When Needed:**

- **Credit Counseling:** If facing challenges, consider seeking assistance from credit counselling agencies for guidance on debt management and credit repair.

- Legal and Financial Consultation: In complex credit scenarios, consult with legal and financial professionals to ensure compliance with regulations and to navigate intricate situations.

Using credit wisely for financial growth requires a strategic and disciplined approach. By understanding the nuances of credit, practicing responsible credit management, and leveraging credit for strategic purposes, you can harness its potential to propel your financial growth and achieve long-term prosperity.

- Breaking the Cycle of Debt

Breaking the cycle of debt is a transformative journey towards financial freedom. It requires a strategic and committed approach to overcome debt challenges and build a solid foundation for a secure financial future. Here's a comprehensive guide to help you break free from the cycle of debt:

1. **Confront Your Financial Reality:**

- **Face Your Debts:** Create a comprehensive list of all your debts, including outstanding balances, interest rates, and minimum monthly payments.

- **Assess Your Spending:** Track your spending to identify areas where you can cut back and allocate more funds towards debt repayment.

2. **Establish a Clear Budget:**

- **Create a Realistic Budget:** Develop a detailed budget that includes all your income, fixed expenses, and discretionary spending.

- **Prioritize Debt Payments:** Allocate a significant portion of your budget to debt repayment, focusing on high-interest debts.

3. **Build an Emergency Fund:**

- **Start Small:** Begin by setting aside a small amount each month to build an emergency fund.

- **Gradual Increase:** As you pay down debts, gradually increase your emergency fund to cover three to six months' worth of living expenses.

4. **Negotiate with Creditors:**

- **Contact Creditors:** Reach out to your creditors to discuss your financial situation. They may be willing to negotiate lower interest rates or more manageable repayment plans.

- **Seek Professional Help:** Consider enlisting the help of credit counselling agencies for professional assistance in negotiating with creditors.

5. **Prioritize High-Interest Debts:**

- **List High-Interest Debts:** Identify debts with the highest interest rates and focus on paying them off first.

- **Snowball or Avalanche Method:** Choose a debt repayment strategy that suits your preferences – whether it's the debt snowball (paying off smallest debts first) or debt avalanche (tackling highest-interest debts first).

6. **Cut Unnecessary Expenses:**

   - **Identify Non-Essentials:** Review your spending habits and cut out non-essential expenses.

   - **Redirect Savings to Debt:** Channel the money saved from cutting expenses directly towards debt repayment.

7. **Explore Debt Consolidation:**

   - **Consolidate High-Interest Debts:** Consider consolidating multiple debts into a single loan with a lower interest rate.

   - **Evaluate Pros and Cons:** Assess the benefits and potential drawbacks of debt consolidation to determine if it aligns with your financial goals.

8. **Financial Education:**

   - **Learn About Personal Finance:** Educate yourself about personal finance, budgeting, and debt management.

   - **Seek Professional Advice:** Consult financial advisors or attend financial education programs to gain insights into effective debt management strategies.

9. Generate Additional Income:

- **Explore Side Hustles:** Identify opportunities for additional income through side hustles or freelance work.

- **Allocate Extra Income to Debt Repayment:** Direct any extra income towards accelerating your debt repayment efforts.

10. Pause New Debt Accumulation:

- **Cut Credit Card Usage:** Temporarily limit the use of credit cards to avoid accumulating new debt.

- **Cash-Only Approach:** Consider adopting a cash-only approach for purchases to promote mindful spending.

11. Create a Debt Repayment Plan:

- **Set Clear Goals:** Define specific and achievable goals for debt repayment.

- **Track Progress:** Regularly monitor your progress and celebrate small victories along the way.

12. Involve Support Systems:

- **Share Your Goals:** Inform friends and family about your debt repayment goals for added accountability.

- **Seek Emotional Support:** If needed, seek emotional support from those close to you or join support groups to connect with others facing similar challenges.

13. Financial Counseling:

- **Explore Professional Help:** Consider engaging the services of financial counsellors who can provide expert guidance on debt management.

- **Debt Management Plans:** Explore debt management plans offered by credit counselling agencies for structured debt repayment.

14. Maintain a Positive Mindset:

- **Focus on Progress:** Celebrate the progress you make, regardless of how small it may seem.

- **Visualize Debt-Free Living:** Maintain a positive vision of a debt-free life and use it as motivation during challenging times.

15. **Celebrate Milestones:**

- **Acknowledge Achievements:** Celebrate reaching milestones in your debt repayment journey.

- **Reinforce Positive Habits:** Use these celebrations as opportunities to reinforce positive financial habits.

16. **Plan for the Future:**

- **Establish Financial Goals:** Set long-term financial goals beyond debt repayment.

- **Build a Savings Plan:** Develop a savings plan to prepare for future expenses and financial goals.

17. **Avoid Relapse:**

- **Practice Financial Discipline:** Once debts are repaid, continue practicing financial discipline to avoid falling back into the cycle of debt.

- **Emergency Fund Maintenance:** Maintain your emergency fund as a buffer against unforeseen financial challenges.

18. **Continuous Improvement:**

- **Review and Adjust Strategies:** Periodically review your financial strategies and adjust them based on changing circumstances.

- **Learn from the Journey:** Reflect on your debt repayment journey to learn valuable lessons about financial management.

Breaking the cycle of debt is a gradual process that requires commitment, discipline, and a strategic approach. By following these steps and staying focused on your financial goals, you can regain control of your finances and pave the way for a debt-free and financially secure future.

CHAPTER 6: CULTIVATING A LEGACY OF PROSPERITY

Welcome to a chapter dedicated to the enduring legacy of prosperity – a chapter that transcends the boundaries of individual financial success and ventures into the realm of creating a lasting impact for generations to come. In the pages that follow, we delve into the art of cultivating wealth not only for personal fulfilment but with the foresight to leave a powerful legacy that extends far beyond our lifetimes.

This chapter is a journey into the deeper significance of financial prosperity – one that extends beyond the accumulation of wealth and delves into the thoughtful, intentional cultivation of a legacy. It explores the idea that true prosperity is not only measured in the wealth amassed but also in the positive influence and opportunities it can provide to future generations.

As we navigate the complexities of financial strategies and wealth-building techniques, we'll intertwine practical advice with the profound notion that our financial decisions today can shape the destinies of those who come after us. This is more than a guide to financial planning; it is an exploration of how our financial choices can become a beacon of empowerment, education, and inspiration for our children, grandchildren, and beyond.

Join us in unravelling the layers of cultivating a legacy of prosperity – from instilling financial wisdom in the younger members of the family to making strategic investments that not only yield returns but contribute to a thriving family heritage. Discover how the choices we make today can echo through the corridors of time, leaving behind a tapestry of abundance, resilience, and empowerment.

So, let's embark on this enlightening journey, exploring the principles and practices that not only build personal wealth but lay the foundation for a legacy that stands as a testament to prosperity, values, and the enduring spirit of financial empowerment. Together, let's cultivate a legacy that transcends generations, creating a tapestry of prosperity that enriches the lives of those who follow in our footsteps.

- Estate Planning for Wealth Preservation

Estate planning is not merely a task for the affluent; it is a strategic and thoughtful endeavor for individuals at every stage of wealth. This chapter delves into the critical realm of estate planning, specifically focusing on the preservation of wealth. As we explore the nuances of this intricate process, we unravel the significance of ensuring that the fruits of one's labor not only endure but continue to flourish for generations to come.

Understanding the Essence of Estate Planning:

Estate planning is often misunderstood as a task reserved for the elderly or the exceptionally wealthy. However, at its core, estate planning is a proactive and comprehensive approach to managing one's assets during their lifetime and beyond. It involves strategic decisions to protect, preserve, and distribute wealth according to one's wishes.

The Imperative of Wealth Preservation:

Preserving wealth is an integral aspect of estate planning, transcending the notion of simple asset distribution. It involves safeguarding the financial legacy you've diligently cultivated, shielding it from unnecessary erosion due to taxes, legal complications, or mismanagement. This chapter explores the strategies and tools at your disposal to ensure that the wealth you pass on remains a source of strength for your heirs.

Key Components of Estate Planning for Wealth Preservation:

1. **Will:** Craft a comprehensive will that clearly outlines how your assets should be distributed. Update it regularly to reflect any changes in your financial situation or family dynamics.

2. **Trusts and Fiduciary Structures:** Explore the benefits of trusts, establishing legal structures that can protect assets, minimize taxes, and ensure a smooth transition of wealth to beneficiaries.

3. **Tax Planning:** Navigate the complexities of tax laws to minimize the impact on your estate. Strategic tax planning can significantly enhance the amount of wealth passed on to your heirs.

4. **Lifetime Giving Strategies:** Consider gifting assets during your lifetime as part of your wealth preservation plan. This not only allows you to witness the impact of your generosity but can also have tax advantages.

5. **Insurance for Estate Liquidity:** Ensure there is sufficient liquidity in your estate to cover any immediate financial needs or tax obligations. Life insurance and other financial instruments can play a crucial role in maintaining liquidity.

6. **Family Governance and Education:** Lay the groundwork for effective wealth management by instilling financial literacy and responsible stewardship in younger family members. Establishing family governance structures can provide a framework for decision-making.

7. **Charitable Giving:** Incorporate philanthropy into your estate planning. Charitable trusts and foundations not only support causes dear to your heart but can also offer tax benefits.

8. **Succession Planning for Family Businesses:** If you own a family business, devise a succession plan that ensures a seamless transition and safeguards the enterprise's financial health.

9. **Healthcare Directives:** Address healthcare decisions in advance through powers of attorney

and advance healthcare directives. This ensures that your medical wishes are respected, preventing financial strain on your estate due to prolonged healthcare expenses.

The Legacy Beyond Finances:

Beyond the tangible assets, this chapter explores the legacy of values and wisdom that you can impart. Effective estate planning encompasses not only the financial aspects but also the preservation of family values, traditions, and the intangible wealth that defines a family's identity.

Consulting Professionals and Evolving Strategies:

Estate planning is not a one-time event but a dynamic process that should evolve with changes in your life, laws, and financial landscape. Consulting with legal and financial professionals is crucial to staying abreast of the latest strategies and ensuring your plan remains aligned with your goals.

A Timeless Legacy of Prosperity:

As we navigate the realm of estate planning for wealth preservation, we recognize that it is a testament to your commitment to the enduring prosperity of your family. This chapter serves as a guide to help you navigate the intricacies of preserving your financial legacy, ensuring that your wealth becomes a source of strength, security, and opportunity for generations to come.

- Creating a Comprehensive Estate Plan

Creating a comprehensive estate plan is a pivotal step in securing your financial legacy and ensuring that your wishes are honored after your passing. This intricate process goes beyond the mere distribution of assets; it involves thoughtful strategies to protect, preserve, and pass on your wealth efficiently. In this exploration of creating a comprehensive estate plan, we unravel the key components and strategic considerations that contribute to a resilient and enduring financial legacy.

1. Self-Assessment and Goal Definition:

- **Reflect on Your Objectives:** Begin by reflecting on your financial and personal objectives. What legacy do you wish to leave behind? What values are essential to preserve?

- **Identify Beneficiaries:** identify beneficiaries and articulate your preferences for asset distribution among family, friends, and charitable causes.

2. Financial Inventory and Valuation:

- **Compile a Detailed Inventory:** List all your assets, including real estate, investments, bank accounts, retirement accounts, life insurance policies, and personal property.

- **Professional Valuation:** Seek professional assistance to accurately value complex assets, such as businesses or unique properties.

3. **Will:**

- **Craft a Comprehensive Will:** Draft a will that clearly outlines your wishes regarding asset distribution, guardianship of minor children, and the appointment of an executor.

- **Regular Updates:** Regularly update your will to accommodate changes in your financial situation, family structure, or legal regulations.

4. **Trusts and Fiduciary Structures:**

- **Explore Trust Options:** Understand the different types of trusts, such as revocable living trusts, irrevocable trusts, and special needs trusts.

- **Align with Objectives:** Establish trusts that align with your specific goals, whether it's minimizing taxes, protecting assets, or ensuring a smooth transfer of wealth.

5. Tax Planning:

- **Understand Tax Implications:** Work with financial advisors to comprehend the tax implications of your estate plan.

- **Utilize Exemptions and Deductions:** Leverage available exemptions and deductions to minimize estate and inheritance taxes.

6. Lifetime Giving Strategies:

- **Gifts and Annual Exclusions:** Strategically use gifts to individuals, taking advantage of annual exclusion limits.

- **Educational and Medical Gifts:** Pay for educational and medical expenses directly to institutions to maximize gifting benefits.

7. Powers of Attorney and Healthcare Directives:

- **Establish Powers of Attorney:** Designate individuals to make financial and legal decisions on your behalf in case of incapacity.

- **Advance Healthcare Directives:** Outline your healthcare preferences and appoint a healthcare proxy to make medical decisions on your behalf.

8. Charitable Giving:

- **Create a Charitable Plan:** Integrate philanthropy into your estate plan through charitable trusts, donor-advised funds, or bequests.

- **Impactful Legacy:** Consider how your charitable contributions can align with your values and leave a lasting impact.

9. Succession Planning for Family Businesses:

- **Define Succession Plans:** If you own a family business, establish a clear succession plan to ensure its continuity.

- **Fair and Transparent Processes:** Consider fair and transparent processes for passing on leadership and ownership to the next generation.

10. Review and Regular Updates:

- **Regularly Review Your Estate Plan:** Conduct periodic reviews to ensure that your estate plan reflects your current financial situation, family dynamics, and legislative changes.

- **Adapt to Life Changes:** Update your estate plan promptly in response to major life events such as births, deaths, marriages, or divorces.

11. Family Governance and Education:

- **Instill Financial Literacy:** Foster financial literacy within the family by providing education on financial management and estate planning.

- **Establish Governance Structures:** Create family governance structures to facilitate decision-making and conflict resolution.

12. Professional Guidance:

- **Legal and Financial Advisors:** Consult with legal and financial professionals who specialize in estate planning.

- **Specialized Advice:** Seek advice on specific considerations, such as international assets, blended families, or complex business structures.

13. Communication with Heirs:

- **Transparent Communication:** Foster open and transparent communication with heirs regarding your estate plan.

- **Prepare Heirs:** Educate heirs about their roles, responsibilities, and the values underpinning the estate plan.

14. Secure Storage and Accessibility:

- **Safe Storage:** Safeguard important documents, including your will and trust documents, in a secure location.

- **Accessibility:** Ensure that designated individuals know where to locate these documents and how to access them when needed.

15. Professional Executor and Trustees:

- Select Competent Executors and Trustees: Choose individuals or professional entities capable of managing the complexities of executing your estate plan.

- Communication with Executors: Communicate your expectations and intentions clearly to those appointed to handle your estate affairs.

16. Legacy beyond Finances:

- Integrate Values and Wisdom: Consider how your estate plan can encapsulate not only financial assets but also the values, stories, and wisdom you wish to pass on.

- Preserving Family Traditions: Identify ways to preserve and pass on cherished family traditions, creating a comprehensive legacy beyond monetary assets.

Creating a comprehensive estate plan is a meticulous process that requires careful consideration of various factors. By incorporating these steps and seeking professional guidance, you can cultivate an estate plan that not only safeguards your financial legacy but also becomes a beacon of empowerment, education, and enduring prosperity for generations to come.

- Minimizing Tax Implications

Estate planning isn't just about preserving and transferring wealth; it's also about strategically minimizing tax implications to ensure that more of your hard-earned assets reach your intended beneficiaries. In this exploration of the process of minimizing tax implications, we delve into effective strategies to optimize your estate plan and reduce the burden of taxes on your legacy.

1. **Understand the Applicable Taxes:**

   - **Estate Tax:** Familiarize yourself with the estate tax, which is a tax on the transfer of property at death. Understand the current exemption limits and tax rates.

   - **Gift Tax:** Consider the implications of the gift tax, which applies to transfers of property during your lifetime. Be aware of annual exclusion limits and lifetime exemption amounts.

2. Leverage the Unified Gift and Estate Tax Exemption:

   - **Maximize Exemptions:** Take advantage of the unified gift and estate tax exemption. As of the latest tax laws, this exemption allows a certain amount of assets to be transferred tax-free during your lifetime and at death.

   - **Spousal Portability**: Explore the option of spousal portability, allowing a surviving spouse to use the unused portion of the deceased spouse's exemption.

3. Strategically Use Annual Exclusions:

- **Gifts within Annual Limits:** Utilize the annual gift tax exclusion to make tax-free gifts up to a certain amount to each recipient.

- **Educational and Medical Exclusions:** Pay educational and medical expenses directly to institutions on behalf of others without it counting toward the annual exclusion limit.

4. **Establish and Fund Irrevocable Trusts:**

- **Irrevocable Life Insurance Trust (ILIT):** Consider creating an ILIT to remove life insurance proceeds from your taxable estate.

- **Grantor Retained Annuity Trust (GRAT):** Use a GRAT to transfer assets to beneficiaries while retaining an annuity for a specified term.

5. **Consider Family Limited Partnerships (FLPs) or Limited Liability Companies (LLCs):**

- **Pooling Family Assets:** Consolidate family assets into FLPs or LLCs, allowing for centralized management and potential valuation discounts for tax purposes.

- **Control and Gifting:** Maintain control of the entities while gifting limited partnership interests to family members.

6. Explore Qualified Personal Residence Trusts (QPRTs):

- **Transfer Primary Residence:** Consider a QPRT to transfer your primary residence or vacation home to an irrevocable trust while retaining the right to live in it for a specified term.

- **Reduced Taxable Value:** This strategy can lead to a reduced taxable value of the residence for gift tax purposes.

7. Utilize Charitable Planning:

- **Charitable Remainder Trust (CRT):** Establish a CRT to provide income to beneficiaries for a specified term, with the remainder going to charity.

- **Charitable Lead Trust (CLT):** Use a CLT to provide income to charities for a set period, after which the remaining assets go to beneficiaries.

8. Maximize Step-Up in Basis:

- **Beneficiary Basis Adjustment:** Assets passing to heirs through the estate receive a step-up in basis to their fair market value at the time of the owner's death.

- **Minimize Capital Gains Tax:** This step-up in basis can significantly minimize capital gains tax for heirs when they sell inherited assets.

9. Coordinate Retirement Account Beneficiary Designations:

- **Strategic Beneficiary Designations:** Plan retirement account beneficiary designations carefully to maximize tax benefits for heirs.

- **Consider Conversions:** Evaluate the potential benefits of converting traditional retirement accounts to Roth accounts for tax-free distributions.

10. **Explore Dynasty Trusts for Generational Wealth:**

- **Preserve Wealth across Generations:** Establishing a dynasty trust allows you to transfer wealth to multiple generations while minimizing transfer taxes.

- **Leverage Generation-Skipping Transfer (GST) Tax Exemption:** Take advantage of the GST tax exemption to allocate assets to grandchildren and beyond without incurring additional transfer taxes.

11. **Stay Informed About Legislative Changes:**

- **Adapt to Legislative Changes:** Keep abreast of changes in tax laws that may impact your estate plan.

- **Consult with Professionals:** Regularly consult with legal and financial professionals to ensure your plan aligns with current regulations.

12. **Consider Life Insurance as a Planning Tool:**

 - **Irrevocable Life Insurance Trust (ILIT):** An ILIT can be used to exclude life insurance proceeds from the taxable estate.

 - **Income Replacement:** Life insurance can serve as a source of income replacement for heirs and offset estate taxes.

13. **Engage in Family Conversations:**

 - **Transparent Communication:** Communicate your estate plan and the reasoning behind it to family members.

 - **Prepare Heirs:** Educate heirs about the potential tax implications of the estate plan and how it may affect them.

14. **Professional Guidance:**

 - **Consult with Tax Professionals:** Seek guidance from tax professionals who specialize in estate planning to optimize your strategies.

- **Regular Reviews:** Conduct regular reviews with professionals to ensure that your plan remains effective in light of changes in tax laws and your financial situation.

15. Evaluate Geographic Considerations:

- **State Estate Taxes:** Be mindful of state estate tax laws, which may have different exemption thresholds and rates.

- **Consider Residency Planning:** Evaluate residency options to minimize exposure to state-level estate taxes.

16. Document and Recordkeeping:

- **Maintain Comprehensive Records:** Keep meticulous records of all financial transactions, gifts, and estate planning documents.

- **Facilitate Smooth Administration:** Well-documented records facilitate a smooth administration of your estate and can be crucial in minimizing potential disputes.

17. **Regularly Review and Adjust:**

- **Periodic Evaluations:** Conduct periodic evaluations of your estate plan, especially when significant life events occur.

- **Adapt to Changing Circumstances:** Adjust your strategies as needed to accommodate changes in tax laws, family dynamics, and financial circumstances.

Minimizing tax implications in your estate plan is a dynamic and strategic process that requires careful consideration, adaptability, and professional expertise. By implementing these strategies and staying proactive in your approach, you can optimize the transfer of your wealth to future generations while minimizing the impact of taxes on your legacy. Always consult with experienced professionals to tailor these strategies to your unique circumstances and ensure compliance with current tax laws.

- Ensuring Smooth Wealth Transfer

Wealth transfer is not just a transaction; it's a profound journey that involves meticulous planning, clear communication, and strategic execution. This process is about passing on not only financial assets but also values, opportunities, and a legacy that endures for generations. In this exploration of ensuring smooth wealth transfer, we delve into the multifaceted strategies that contribute to a seamless transition of wealth from one generation to the next.

1. **Define Your Legacy and Objectives:**

- **Clarify Intentions:** Clearly articulate your values, intentions, and objectives for the wealth you are passing on.

- **Identify Key Priorities:** Determine the key priorities such as supporting family members, charitable causes, or specific financial goals.

2. Open and Transparent Communication:

- **Family Discussions:** Initiate open discussions with family members about the wealth transfer plan.

- **Explain Decision-Making**: Communicate the rationale behind your decisions and how they align with your values.

3. Create a Comprehensive Estate Plan:

- **Wills and Trusts:** Craft a well-structured will and consider the use of trusts to provide detailed instructions for wealth distribution.

- **Professional Guidance:** Seek professional advice to ensure your estate plan aligns with legal requirements and your specific goals.

4. Provide Financial Education:

- **Family Financial Literacy:** Equip heirs with financial literacy to empower them to manage and grow inherited wealth.

- **Educational Programs:** Consider implementing educational programs or engaging financial advisors to provide ongoing guidance.

5. Address Family Dynamics:

- **Potential Conflicts:** Anticipate potential conflicts and address them proactively within the estate plan.

- **Mediation Services:** Consider involving professional mediators to facilitate family discussions and conflict resolution.

6. Establish Family Governance Structures:

- **Family Meetings:** Schedule regular family meetings to discuss financial matters, goals, and plans.

- **Create Family Councils:** Establish family councils or committees to oversee specific aspects of wealth management.

7. Succession Planning for Family Businesses:

- **Leadership Transition:** Develop a comprehensive succession plan for family businesses to ensure a smooth transition of leadership.

- **Skill and Knowledge Transfer:** Facilitate the transfer of skills and knowledge from one generation to the next.

8. Encourage Entrepreneurship and Innovation:

- **Foster Entrepreneurial Spirit:** Encourage family members to explore entrepreneurial ventures and innovative projects.

- **Seed Capital:** Provide seed capital for business ideas within the family to promote financial independence.

9. Consider Philanthropy:

- **Charitable Giving:** Integrate philanthropy into your wealth transfer plan by allocating funds to charitable causes.

- **Establish Family Foundations:** Create family foundations or charitable trusts to involve the family in philanthropic efforts.

10. **Plan for Special Circumstances:**

- **Special Needs**: If applicable, create trusts or provisions for family members with special needs.

- **Educational Support:** Designate funds for educational expenses and career development.

11. **Regularly Review and Update the Plan:**

- **Life Changes:** Regularly review and update your estate plan in response to life events such as marriages, births, or deaths.

- **Adapt to Changing Circumstances:** Be flexible and adapt your plan to changes in tax laws, economic conditions, and family dynamics.

12. **Professional Advisors and Executors:**

- **Select Competent Advisors:** Choose professional advisors who specialize in wealth transfer and family governance.

- **Clear Instructions:** Provide clear instructions to executors and trustees to facilitate the implementation of your wealth transfer plan.

13. Financial Security for Surviving Spouses:

- **Spousal Support:** Ensure that surviving spouses are financially secure with provisions for living expenses and healthcare.

- **Asset Management:** Guide managing assets and financial decision-making.

14. Explore Life Insurance as a Tool:

- **Liquidity Needs:** Consider life insurance to provide liquidity for estate taxes and immediate financial needs.

- **Equalization of Inheritances:** Use life insurance to equalize inheritances among heirs with diverse assets.

15. Address International Considerations:

- **Tax Implications:** Be aware of potential tax implications in multiple jurisdictions if family members reside in different countries.

- **Legal Expertise:** Seek legal expertise to navigate international laws governing wealth transfer.

16. Document and Organize Information:

- **Centralized Documentation:** Keep a centralized and organized record of all financial information, legal documents, and key contacts.

- **Facilitate Executor Responsibilities:** This aids executors in efficiently managing the estate.

17. Facilitate Smooth Business Transition:

   - Business Continuity Plan: Establish a business continuity plan for family businesses, detailing the transition of leadership and operations.

   - Employee and Customer Communication: Communicate the transition plan to employees and customers to maintain stability.

Ensuring a smooth wealth transfer is a holistic process that involves a combination of legal, financial, and interpersonal strategies. By proactively addressing potential challenges, fostering transparent communication, and implementing a well-thought-out estate plan, you can pave the way for a seamless transition of wealth that aligns with your values and aspirations. Continual adaptation, open dialogue, and collaboration with professional advisors are key elements in building a lasting legacy that stands the test of time.

- Philanthropy and Giving Back

Philanthropy is not just an act of generosity; it's a transformative force that has the power to create lasting change in the world. In this exploration of philanthropy and giving back, we delve into the profound impact of charitable endeavors, how they contribute to personal fulfilment, and how philanthropy can be integrated into a comprehensive wealth management strategy.

1. **The Essence of Philanthropy:**

- **Beyond Financial Contributions:** Philanthropy extends beyond monetary donations; it encompasses a commitment to making a positive impact on society.

- **Strategic Giving:** Engage in strategic giving by aligning charitable efforts with personal values and societal needs.

2. Integration into Wealth Management:

- **Holistic Wealth:** Philanthropy is a pillar of holistic wealth management, emphasizing the importance of financial, social, and emotional well-being.

- **Fulfillment and Purpose:** The act of giving back adds a layer of fulfilment and purpose to wealth creation.

3. Identifying Passionate Causes:

- **Personal Values:** Identify causes aligned with personal values, passions, and areas where meaningful change can be achieved.

- **Research and Due Diligence:** Conduct thorough research to ensure that chosen charities are reputable, effective, and aligned with philanthropic goals.

4. Establishing a Philanthropic Vision:

- **Define Objectives:** Clearly define philanthropic objectives and the desired impact on the community or cause.

- **Long-Term Vision:** Develop a long-term vision for sustained impact, recognizing that philanthropy is an ongoing commitment.

5. **Creating Family Foundations and Trusts:**

- **Legacy Planning:** Establish family foundations or charitable trusts to involve multiple generations in philanthropy.

- **Educational Opportunities:** Use these structures as educational platforms, instilling philanthropic values in younger family members.

6. **Strategic Grantmaking:**

- **Needs Assessment:** Conduct a needs assessment to identify areas where financial support can have the most significant impact.

- **Collaborative Approaches:** Explore collaborative approaches by partnering with other philanthropists, organizations, or governments to amplify impact.

7. Measuring Impact:

- Quantitative and Qualitative Metrics: Develop metrics to measure both quantitative and qualitative impact.

- Adaptive Strategies: Be willing to adapt philanthropic strategies based on ongoing evaluations and changing circumstances.

8. Engaging in Social Entrepreneurship:

- Innovative Solutions: Support social entrepreneurs and innovative solutions that address systemic issues.

- Sustainable Change: Social entrepreneurship combines business principles with social impact, contributing to sustainable change.

9. Involving the Next Generation:

- **Philanthropic Education**: Educate younger family members about the importance of philanthropy and involve them in decision-making.

- **Passing on Values:** Use philanthropy as a means to pass on family values and a sense of responsibility to future generations.

10. Collaborating with Nonprofits:

- **Transparent Communication:** Establish transparent communication with nonprofit partners, fostering trust and collaboration.

- **Capacity Building:** Go beyond financial support by providing capacity-building assistance to nonprofits for long-term sustainability.

11. Creating Impactful Partnerships:

- **Strategic Alliances:** Form strategic alliances with other philanthropists, corporations, and NGOs to create synergies.

- **Maximizing Resources:** Collaborate to maximize the impact of resources and tackle complex challenges more effectively.

12. Leveraging Technology for Social Good:

- **Digital Platforms:** Utilize technology and digital platforms to amplify the reach of philanthropic efforts.

- **Crowdsourced Initiatives:** Engage in crowdsourced initiatives that leverage the power of the community for social good.

13. Ethical Considerations:

- **Ethical and Responsible Giving:** Ensure that philanthropy is conducted ethically, with a focus on responsible giving.

- **Social and Environmental Impact:** Consider the broader social and environmental impact of philanthropic activities.

14. **Building a Legacy of Impact:**

- **Enduring Impact:** Philanthropy is a means to build a legacy of impact that extends beyond one's lifetime.

- **Inspiring Others:** By leading with philanthropy, individuals can inspire others to contribute to the greater good.

15. **Global Philanthropy:**

- **International Contributions:** Consider the global impact of philanthropy, addressing issues that transcend national boundaries.

- **Cultural Sensitivity:** Approach global philanthropy with cultural sensitivity, understanding local contexts and needs.

16. **Personal Growth and Fulfillment:**

- **Personal Transformation:** Engaging in philanthropy often leads to personal transformation and a deep sense of fulfilment.

- **Connection to Community:** Establishing connections with communities and individuals being served fosters a sense of shared humanity.

Philanthropy and giving back are not just about financial transactions; they are about creating a meaningful and enduring legacy. By integrating philanthropy into wealth management strategies, individuals have the opportunity to make a positive impact on the world, inspire future generations, and cultivate a legacy that goes beyond monetary wealth. Whether through strategic grant making, collaborative initiatives, or social entrepreneurship, philanthropy is a powerful force for positive change that transcends individual success and contributes to the well-being of society at large.

- Making a Positive Impact on the World

Making a positive impact on the world is a noble endeavor that goes beyond individual success, transcending personal goals to contribute to the well-being of communities and the planet. In this exploration of the process of making a positive impact, we delve into the principles, strategies, and actions that individuals and organizations can undertake to create meaningful change and leave a lasting legacy.

1. **Clarifying Your Values and Vision:**

- **Self-Reflection:** Begin by reflecting on your values, beliefs, and the kind of world you envision.

- **Define Your Vision:** Clearly articulate your vision for the positive impact you want to make, considering both short-term and long-term goals.

2. **Identifying Areas of Impact:**

- **Assess Global and Local Needs:** Conduct a thorough assessment of global and local challenges to identify areas where your efforts can make a meaningful difference.

- **Personal Passion Alignment:** Align your areas of impact with your passions and skills to maximize effectiveness.

3. Setting Clear and Measurable Goals:

- **SMART Goals:** Establish Specific, Measurable, Achievable, Relevant, and Time-Bound (SMART) goals for your impact initiatives.

- **Quantifiable Metrics:** Define quantifiable metrics to assess progress and success.

4. Engaging in Social Entrepreneurship:

- **Innovative Solutions:** Consider social entrepreneurship as a means to address social and environmental challenges through innovative, sustainable business models.

- **Triple Bottom Line:** Embrace the triple bottom line approach, considering social, environmental, and financial impacts.

5. Leveraging Technology for Good:

- **Tech for Social Impact:** Utilize technology as a tool for positive change, whether through creating innovative solutions or leveraging digital platforms for awareness and collaboration.

- **Digital Inclusion:** Ensure that your initiatives consider digital inclusion to reach diverse communities.

6. Collaborating with Like-Minded Partners:

- **Strategic Alliances:** Form partnerships with individuals, organizations, and institutions that share a similar commitment to positive impact.

- **Collective Strength:** Collaborate to amplify efforts, share resources, and collectively address complex challenges.

7. Engaging in Advocacy and Awareness:

- **Raise Awareness:** Advocate for causes that align with your mission, leveraging your voice and influence.

- **Educational Initiatives:** Contribute to educational initiatives that promote awareness and understanding of critical issues.

8. Sustainable Environmental Practices:

- **Eco-Friendly Choices:** Make sustainable choices in personal and organizational practices to minimize environmental impact.

- **Carbon Footprint Reduction:** Explore ways to reduce carbon footprint through energy efficiency, conservation, and renewable energy.

9. **Philanthropy and Charitable Giving:**

- **Strategic Philanthropy:** Engage in strategic philanthropy by supporting causes aligned with your values and vision.

- **Impactful Giving:** Prioritize giving that has a tangible and sustainable impact on communities and individuals.

10. **Volunteerism and Community Engagement:**

- **Hands-On Involvement:** Actively participate in volunteer initiatives to directly engage with communities and contribute your time and skills.

- **Local Empowerment:** Focus on empowering local communities through collaborative efforts and inclusive engagement.

11. Social Impact Investing:

- **Investing with Purpose:** Consider social impact investing, directing funds toward businesses and projects that generate positive social and environmental outcomes.

- **Balancing Returns and Impact:** Seek a balance between financial returns and the impact of your investments.

12. Mentorship and Skill-Sharing:

- **Transfer of Knowledge**: Contribute to positive impact by mentoring and sharing skills with individuals, especially those in underserved communities.

- **Capacity Building:** Empower others to build their capacities and become agents of change.

13. Advocating for Social Justice:

- **Equity and Inclusion:** Advocate for social justice, equity, and inclusion in all aspects of life.

- **Addressing Systemic Issues:** Work towards systemic change to eradicate inequalities and promote a fair and just society.

14. Continuous Learning and Adaptation:

- **Stay Informed:** Stay informed about evolving global and local challenges to adapt your strategies accordingly.

- **Embrace a Growth Mindset:** Cultivate a growth mindset that embraces learning from successes and failures.

15. Fostering Global Citizenship:

- **Cultural Sensitivity:** Approach impact initiatives with cultural sensitivity and an understanding of diverse perspectives.

- **Global Collaboration:** Foster a sense of global citizenship by collaborating with individuals and organizations worldwide.

16. Inspiring Others to Act:

- **Lead by Example:** Inspire others through your actions, demonstrating that positive impact is achievable and meaningful.

- **Educational Outreach:** Share your experiences and insights through educational platforms to encourage others to join the cause.

17. Measuring and Communicating Impact:

- **Impact Assessment:** Regularly assess and measure the impact of your initiatives against established goals.

- **Transparent Reporting**: Communicate impact transparently to build trust with stakeholders and inspire confidence in your efforts.

Making a positive impact on the world is a multifaceted journey that involves passion, strategic thinking, and a commitment to continuous improvement. By aligning personal values with meaningful goals, leveraging resources wisely, and engaging with others in collaborative efforts, individuals and organizations can contribute to building a better, more sustainable future for all. Whether through philanthropy, entrepreneurship, advocacy, or volunteerism, the collective efforts of those dedicated to positive impact have the potential to create a ripple effect that extends far beyond individual actions.

- Aligning Philanthropy with Personal Values

Philanthropy becomes most meaningful and impactful when it aligns with an individual's or organizations deeply held values. Crafting a purpose-driven giving strategy involves a thoughtful process that ensures the resources contributed not only make a positive impact on the world but also resonate with the core beliefs and principles of the giver. Here's a guide to the process of aligning philanthropy with personal values:

1. Self-Reflection and Values Clarification:

- **Introspection:** Begin with introspective self-reflection to identify your core values, beliefs, and passions.

- **Values Clarification:** Clearly articulate the principles that guide your life and the causes that resonate with your deepest convictions.

2. Identify Key Areas of Personal Passion:

- **Passion Alignment:** Identify specific areas or causes that ignite passion and align with your core values.

- **Emotional Connection:** Seek causes that create a profound emotional connection, driving a sustained commitment to making a difference.

3. **Research and Understand Causes:**

- **In-Depth Exploration:** Conduct thorough research on potential causes, organizations, and initiatives.

- Impact Assessment: Evaluate the impact of different causes to ensure they align with your intended outcomes and resonate with your values.

4. **Define Clear Philanthropic Objectives:**

- **SMART Goals:** Establish Specific, Measurable, Achievable, Relevant, and Time-Bound (SMART) philanthropic goals.

- **Long-Term Vision:** Develop a long-term vision that reflects your commitment to sustained positive impact.

5. **Consider the Scope of Impact:**

- **Local, National, or Global:** Determine the geographical scope of your philanthropic efforts, whether they are local, national, or global.

- **Communities Served:** Understand the communities and populations that your chosen causes aim to serve.

6. Collaborate with Like-Minded Organizations:

- **Shared Values:** Seek collaborations with organizations that share similar values and a commitment to your chosen causes.

- **Mutual Goals:** Collaborate to amplify impact and contribute to shared objectives.

7. Evaluate Organizational Practices:

- **Ethical Considerations:** Ensure that the organizations you support adhere to ethical practices and values.

- **Transparent Operations:** Choose organizations that are transparent in their operations and impact reporting.

8. Create a Personalized Giving Plan:

- **Diversification:** Develop a giving plan that diversifies support across different causes or organizations that align with various aspects of your values.

- **Strategic Allocation:** Allocate resources strategically, considering the unique needs and challenges of each cause.

9. Engage in Hands-On Philanthropy:

- **Active Participation:** Consider hands-on engagement with causes, volunteering time, and actively participating in initiatives.

- **Direct Impact:** Direct involvement fosters a deeper connection with the cause and allows for firsthand understanding of the impact.

10. Incorporate Feedback Mechanisms:

- **Stakeholder Input:** Establish mechanisms for receiving feedback from beneficiaries, communities, and stakeholders.

- **Adaptive Strategies:** Use feedback to adapt and refine your philanthropic strategies for increased effectiveness.

11. Flexibility and Adaptability:

- **Changing Needs:** Remain flexible and adaptable to changing social, economic, and environmental needs.

- **Emerging Issues:** Be open to supporting emerging issues that align with your values and require immediate attention.

12. Educate and Involve Family Members:

- **Family Values:** If applicable, involve family members in the philanthropic process, ensuring alignment with shared family values.

- **Generational Legacy:** Use philanthropy as a means to pass on values to future generations.

13. **Measure and Communicate Impact:**

- **Impact Metrics:** Establish clear metrics to measure the impact of your philanthropic endeavors.

- **Transparent Communication:** Communicate impact transparently, sharing successes, challenges, and lessons learned with stakeholders.

14. **Stay Informed and Evolve:**

- **Continuous Learning:** Stay informed about evolving issues, trends, and best practices in the philanthropic landscape.

- **Adaptive Strategies:** Adapt your giving strategy based on new information and a continually evolving understanding of the social and environmental challenges.

15. **Foster a Personal Connection:**

- **Emotional Engagement**: Cultivate a personal connection with the causes you support, ensuring that your philanthropy is driven by genuine passion and commitment.

- **Storytelling:** Share compelling stories that reflect the human impact of your philanthropic efforts, creating an emotional bond with your audience.

16. Regularly Review and Revise:

- **Periodic Evaluations:** Conduct periodic evaluations of your giving strategy to ensure ongoing alignment with your values.

- **Strategic Adjustments:** Make strategic adjustments as needed to address emerging priorities or shifts in personal values.

17. Seek Professional Guidance:

- **Philanthropy Advisors:** If needed, seek advice from philanthropy advisors who can provide insights into effective giving strategies aligned with your values.

- Legal and Financial Professionals: Consult with legal and financial professionals to ensure compliance with regulations and maximize the impact of your philanthropy.

Aligning philanthropy with personal values is a transformative journey that deepens the impact of charitable efforts. By integrating values, passion, and a strategic approach, individuals and organizations can create a legacy of purposeful giving that not only makes a positive difference in the world but also reflects the essence of who they are. As a dynamic and evolving process, aligning philanthropy with personal values ensures that each contribution is a meaningful step toward creating a better, more compassionate world.

- Incorporating Giving into Your Financial Plan

Integrating philanthropy into your financial plan is a transformative endeavor that allows you to allocate resources not just for personal wealth accumulation

but also for making a positive impact on the world.
Here's a comprehensive guide to the process of
incorporating giving into your financial plan:

1. **Define Your Philanthropic Vision and Values:**

   - **Values Alignment:** Align your giving strategy
with your core values, ensuring that your
philanthropy reflects your principles.

   - **Long-Term Vision:** Establish a long-term
vision for your philanthropic endeavors, considering
the legacy you want to leave and the impact you
hope to achieve.

2. **Assess Your Financial Capacity:**

   - **Budget Allocation:** Evaluate your financial
capacity to determine a realistic percentage or fixed
amount of your income or assets dedicated to
philanthropy.

   - **Impactful Giving:** Strive for a balance that
allows for impactful giving without compromising
your financial well-being.

3. **Set Clear and Measurable Giving Goals:**

- **SMART Goals:** Establish Specific, Measurable, Achievable, Relevant, and Time-Bound (SMART) philanthropic goals.

- **Quantifiable Metrics:** Define clear metrics to measure the success and impact of your giving initiatives.

4. **Identify Causes and Organizations:**

- **Research and Due Diligence:** Conduct thorough research on causes and organizations that align with your values and mission.

- **Diversification:** Consider supporting a variety of causes to address diverse societal needs.

5. **Incorporate Giving Categories:**

- **Strategic Categories:** Categorize your giving based on strategic priorities, such as education, healthcare, poverty alleviation, or environmental conservation.

- Emergency Relief: Allocate funds for emergency relief efforts, providing flexibility to respond to unforeseen crises.

6. Create a Giving Plan:

- Annual Giving Plan: Develop an annual giving plan outlining the allocation of funds to specific causes and organizations.

- Multi-Year Commitments: Consider making multi-year commitments to provide sustained support for long-term projects.

7. Explore Different Giving Vehicles:

- Donor-Advised Funds: Consider establishing a donor-advised fund for centralized and tax-efficient giving.

- Charitable Trusts: Explore charitable remainder trusts or charitable lead trusts for more complex giving structures.

8. Integrate Giving with Financial Milestones:

- **Life Events:** Integrate philanthropy into significant life events such as birthdays, anniversaries, or major career achievements.

- **Financial Windfalls:** Develop a plan for philanthropy when experiencing financial windfalls, ensuring a thoughtful and impactful allocation.

9. Engage Family Members:

- **Family Philanthropy:** Involve family members in the philanthropic decision-making process, fostering shared values and a sense of responsibility.

- **Educational Initiatives:** Use philanthropy as an educational tool for younger family members to learn about social responsibility.

10. Explore Matching Gift Programs:

- **Corporate Matching:** Leverage corporate matching gift programs if available, maximizing the impact of your contributions.

- **Encourage Workplace Giving:** Encourage colleagues or employees to participate in workplace giving initiatives.

11. Attend Philanthropic Events and Conferences:

- **Networking:** Attend events and conferences focused on philanthropy to network with like-minded individuals and learn about innovative initiatives.

- **Educational Opportunities:** Stay informed about evolving trends and best practices in the philanthropic sector.

12. Consider Impact Investing:

- **Socially Responsible Investments:** Explore impact investing, allocating a portion of your investment portfolio to socially responsible assets.

- **Balancing Returns and Impact:** Strive for a balance between financial returns and the social or environmental impact of your investments.

13. **Review and Adjust Your Giving Strategy**:

- **Regular Assessments:** Periodically assess the impact of your giving strategy against established goals.

- **Adapt to Changing Circumstances:** Be flexible and adjust your giving strategy in response to changing circumstances or emerging needs.

14. **Tax Planning for Philanthropy:**

- **Tax-Efficient Giving:** Work with financial advisors to optimize your tax position through strategic philanthropic planning.

- **Maximize Deductions:** Understand the tax benefits associated with charitable giving and maximize deductions within legal frameworks.

15. **Promote Transparency and Accountability:**

- **Impact Reporting:** Encourage organizations to provide transparent impact reports on the use of funds.

- **Accountability:** Prioritize organizations with strong accountability structures to ensure effective use of resources.

16. Celebrate Philanthropic Milestones:

- **Recognition:** Celebrate milestones in your philanthropic journey, acknowledging the positive impact achieved.

- **Inspiration:** Share your philanthropic journey to inspire others and encourage collective action.

17. Seek Professional Advice:

- **Philanthropy Advisors:** Consult with philanthropy advisors for expert guidance on optimizing your giving strategy.

- **Legal and Financial Professionals:** Collaborate with legal and financial professionals to ensure compliance and maximize the impact of your philanthropy.

 Incorporating giving into your financial plan is a holistic and purposeful process that enriches both your financial well-being and your positive impact on the world. By aligning your giving strategy with personal values, setting clear goals, and exploring diverse giving vehicles, you can create a philanthropic blueprint that resonates with your unique vision for a better, more compassionate world. As a dynamic and evolving journey, incorporating giving into your financial plan ensures that your wealth is not just a measure of success but a tool for meaningful and lasting change.

CONCLUSION

As we reach the culmination of our journey together in "How to Manage Your Money Like a Millionaire," it is with a sense of empowerment and newfound financial wisdom that you stand at the threshold of a transformed financial future. This book has been a guide, a companion, and a roadmap to not just accumulating wealth but mastering the art of managing it with the finesse of those who have achieved financial greatness.

Throughout these pages, we've delved into the intricate dance between mindset and money, explored the psychology of wealth, and embraced the strategies that millionaires use to navigate the financial landscape. From cultivating a millionaire mindset to crafting a personalized financial blueprint, you've embarked on a transformative experience that extends beyond dollars and cents—

it's about cultivating a mindset of abundance, resilience, and purpose.

As you reflect on the lessons learned, remember that managing your money like a millionaire is not a static destination but a dynamic journey. It's about continual learning, adaptability to change, and the courage to embrace opportunities. Let these principles be the foundation upon which you build a life of financial abundance, security, and fulfilment.

In the chapters on overcoming limiting beliefs, visualizing financial success, and embracing risk and opportunity, you've discovered the powerful tools that can reshape your financial reality. You've learned that a can-do attitude, coupled with a strategic approach, can turn obstacles into stepping stones and setbacks into comebacks.

Crafting your financial blueprint involves setting SMART goals, defining objectives aligned with your values, and establishing measurable milestones. It's about aligning your financial choices with the life you envision, recognizing that every decision today shapes the wealth of tomorrow.

Mastering the art of budgeting and saving, you've not only learned to distinguish between essentials and luxuries but also discovered the significance of building an emergency fund and planning for major expenses. You've embraced the delicate balance between enjoying the present and ensuring financial responsibility, all while maximizing savings through smart banking and leveraging technology for efficiency.

The journey through the world of investments demystified the complexities, from investment basics to stocks, bonds, and beyond. By understanding risk tolerance, and diversification, and choosing investments aligned with your goals, you've unlocked the doors to building a diversified investment portfolio. Real estate investments, entrepreneurship, and exploring alternative investment avenues have all become integral parts of your wealth-building arsenal.

Crushing debt and supercharging your wealth requires a strategic approach. You've learned not just to eliminate debt efficiently but to turn it into an opportunity for wealth-building. By negotiating favorable terms, prioritizing high-interest debts, and using credit wisely, you've harnessed the power to break free from the cycle of debt and leverage it strategically for financial growth.

As we venture into the realm of cultivating a legacy of prosperity, we explore estate planning, minimizing tax implications, and ensuring a smooth wealth transfer. The chapters on philanthropy and giving back underscore the profound impact generosity can have, not only on the recipients but also on your fulfilment and the legacy you leave behind.

In every step, you've been guided by the principle that making a positive impact on the world is not just a noble pursuit but an integral part of managing wealth like a millionaire. By aligning philanthropy with personal values, incorporating giving into your financial plan, and actively seeking ways to create a positive impact, you've become a steward of not just financial success but of shared prosperity.

Now, armed with knowledge, fortified by a millionaire mindset, and inspired by the limitless possibilities that financial mastery brings, you are ready to embark on your journey of wealth creation, purposeful giving, and enduring prosperity. May the principles you've embraced in these pages be the stepping stones to a life where your financial potential knows no bounds?

In closing, remember that managing your money like a millionaire is not merely a goal; it's a lifestyle, a mindset, and a commitment to continual growth. Your journey has just begun, and the pages of your financial story await the exciting chapters that lie ahead. Unleash your financial potential, live with purpose, and let the legacy you create be a testament to the extraordinary impact of managing your money like a millionaire.

www.ingramcontent.com/pod-product-compliance
Lightning Source LLC
Chambersburg PA
CBHW070107260726
48658CB00001B/12